KV-510-393

Contents

Editor's preface

This book forms part of a series entitled Issues in Sociology which is designed for students on A Level and other similar courses in schools and colleges.

The series consists of a set of relatively short books, intended for personal use by the student, which can provide a more flexible and stimulating programme of study than is offered by the conventional textbook alone.

Each book covers one key substantive area of current A Level syllabuses. The series aims particularly to cover those topics that are new and popular, or those that are inadequately provided for in existing texts. It also provides a different approach from that of the textbook in that, rather than being presented with a digest of sociological literature and concerns, students will confront a selection of original extracts from such literature which they will analyse and assess for themselves. The aim is to emphasise the nature of sociological enquiry and debate and to encourage students to interpret and assess the evidence and arguments put forward.

The intention of this series, therefore, is not to replace the textbook approach but rather to supplement and extend it.

The author's introduction outlines the field of study covered by the book, placing it in its wider context and highlighting a number of general issues and problems. Each chapter consists primarily of a series of documentary extracts focusing on a particular issue or area of debate and a short introduction sets out a framework within which the student can read and analyse the material presented. Each extract is selected to illustrate a particular source of data or perspective and to complement each by providing alternative views or contrasting evidence.

Questions are supplied that test the full range of skills from comprehension of specific extracts to synthesis and appraisal of a range of literature as required in essay questions in A Level and equivalent examinations.

Finally, there is a list of references for parallel or follow-up reading by students at the end of each chapter.

R.O.

ISSUES IN SOCIOLOGY

BOOK LOAN

Please return or renew it no later
than the last date shown below

ISSUES IN SOCIOLOGY
Edited by Robin Oakley

EDUCATION, SCHOOLS AND SCHOOLING

Robert G. Burgess

Senior Lecturer in Sociology, University of Warwick

Macmillan Education

First published 1985

Published by
MACMILLAN EDUCATION LTD
Houndmills, Basingstoke, Hampshire RG21 2XS
and London
Companies and representatives
throughout the world

Typeset by Columns, Reading
Printed in Hong Kong

British Library Cataloguing in Publication Data
Burgess, Robert G.
Education, schools and schooling. — (Issues
in sociology; 4)
1. Educational sociology
I. Title   II. Series
370.19   LC191
ISBN 0–333–37421–5

\

Acknowledgements

In the course of producing this book I have been fortunate to have the help and support of the series editor, Robin Oakley, who has provided many useful suggestions. In addition, Liz Griffiths and Marie Stowell commented on an earlier draft of this manuscript based on their experience of teaching the sociology of education for the Advanced Level GCE examinations, while Hilary Burgess provided much help, advice and encouragement for which I am very grateful. Last, but by no means least, Hilary Bayliss cheerfully typed and retyped copies of the manuscript with great efficiency.

R.G.B.

The author and publishers wish to thank the following, who have kindly given permission for the use of copyright material:

George Allen & Unwin (Publishers) Ltd for extracts from *The Diploma Disease: Education, Qualification and Development* (1976) by Ronald Dore, and from *Equality* (fifth edition, 1964), by R. H. Tawney.
    Associated Book Publishers Ltd for extracts from *Knowledge, Education and Schooling* by R. K. Brown, published by Tavistock Publications; from *Interaction in the Classroom* by Sara Delamont, published by Methuen & Company; from *The Sociology of School Organisation* by R. King, published by Methuen & Company; from *Experiencing Comprehensive Education* by R. G. Burgess, published by Methuen & Company; and from *Language, Schools and Classrooms* by M. Stubbs, published by Methuen & Company.
    Basil Blackwell Limited for an extract from *The Poverty of Education: A Study in the Politics of Opportunity* (1975) by D. Byrne, B. Williamson and B. Fletcher.
    British Sociological Association for an extract from 'After sixteen: what choice?' by Helen Roberts in *Exploring Society* edited by R. G. Burgess.
    Cambridge University Press for extracts from *Deschooling: A Reader* by Ian Lister, and from *Beachside Comprehensive: A Case Study of Secondary Schooling* by S. J. Ball.
    The Controller of Her Majesty's Stationery Office for extracts from Crown copyright material.
    Croom Helm Ltd for extracts from *Pupil Strategies: Explorations in the Sociology of the School* by S. J. Ball; *School Subjects and Curriculum Change* by I. F. Goodson and from *Contemporary Education Policy* by J. Beck.
    Falmer Press Ltd for an extract from *Defining the Curriculum* edited by I. F. Goodson and S. J. Ball.
    Gower Publishing Company Ltd for an extract from *Learning to Labour* by Paul Willis.
    Haslingfield United Charities for 'Rules of the Haslingfield National School' Document No. R59/27/3/3 in the County Record Office, Cambridge.
    Heinemann Educational Books for extracts from *The Language of Teaching* by A. D. Edwards and V. J. Furlong, and *Disadvantage and Education* by J. Mortimore and T. Blackstone.
    William Heinemann Ltd for an extract from *All Our Future* by J. W. B. Douglas, J. M. Ross and H. R. Simpson.

Hodder & Stoughton Educational for an extract from *A Question of Schooling* edited by J. E. C. Macbeath.

Longman Group Ltd for an extract from *Education as Social Policy* by J. Finch.

Macmillan Publishing Co. Inc. for extracts from *Education and Sociology* by Emile Durkheim, translated by Sherwood D. Fox, copyright 1956 by The Free Press, and from *Education, Economy and Society* edited by A. H. Halsey, J. Flood and C. A. Anderson, copyright 1961 by The Free Press.

Manchester University Press for extracts from *Hightown Grammar: The School as a Social System*, by Colin Lacy, and from *The Missing Half: Girls and Science Education* by David Newbold.

The NFER-Nelson Publishing Company for an extract from *Ability Grouping – the Banbury Enquiry* by D. Newbold.

The Open University Press for an extract from 'Education and the labour market' by D. Finn and S. Frith, in *The State and the Politics of Education*, Block 1, Part 2, Unit 4, 1981.

Oxford University Press for extracts from *Change in British Society* by A. H. Halsey (1978); and from *Origins and Destinations: Family, Class and Education in Modern Britain* by A. H. Halsey, A. F. Heath and J. M. Ridge (1980).

Oxford University Press Inc. for an extract from *Power and Ideology in Education* by J. Karabel and A. H. Halsey.

Penguin Books Ltd for extracts from *Letter to a Teacher* by The School of Barbiana (Penguin Education Special, 1970) © 1969 by School of Barbiana, translation © 1970 by Random House, Inc., from 'Elites versus equals: the political background to the comprehensive reform' by Caroline Benn from *Education and Equality* edited by David Rubinstein (Penguin Education 1979). Copyright © 1979 Caroline Benn; and from *Class in a Capitalist Society* by John Westergaard and Henrietta Resler (Pelican Books, 1976). Copyright © 1975 by John Westergaard and Henrietta Resler.

David Reynolds for an extract from his review of *Fifteen Thousand Hours* in *British Journal of Sociology of Education*, vol. 1, no. 2 (1980).

Routledge & Kegan Paul for extracts from *Social Relations in a Secondary School* by D. H. Hargreaves; *The Challenge for the Comprehensive School* by D. H. Hargreaves; *Deviance in Classrooms* by D. H. Hargreaves, S. K. Hester and F. J. Mellor; *Teachers and Classes: A Marxist Analysis* by K. Harris; *The Sociology of Educational Ideas* by J. Evetts; *The Universities and British Industry* by M. Sanderson; *Women and Schooling* by R. Deem; *The Divided School* by P. Woods; *Schooling in Capitalist America* by S. Bowles and H. Gintis, and *Schooling for Women's Work* by R. Deem.

Times Newspapers Ltd for an extract from the article by Tessa Blackstone in *The Times Higher Educational Supplement* (1980).

Barry Troyna for an extract from his article in *The Social Sciences in Educational Studies* (1982).

University of London Institute of Education for an extract from *Girls and Mathematics: The Early Years* by R. Walden and V. Walkerdine (Bedford Way Papers 8).

The Women's Press Ltd for an extract from *Learning to Lose: Sexism and Education* edited by Dale Spender and Elizabeth Sarah.

Questions from past examination papers have been kindly supplied by the following boards: Associated Examining Board; Joint Matriculation Board; University of London; and University of Oxford Delegacy of Local Examinations.

Every effort has been made to trace all the copyright holders but if any have been inadvertently overlooked the publishers will be pleased to make the necessary arrangements at the first opportunity.

Introduction

The shape, substance and style of the sociology of education has undergone considerable change in the last thirty years. In part these changes are a reflection of changes in the discipline of sociology, with its shifting interests in theories and methods, which have been taken up and used by researchers in many sub-disciplines, including the sociology of education. In turn, sociologists have responded to changes that have occurred in educational systems such as the English system, where they have been involved in debates concerning the relationship between school and work, patterns of schooling especially in the secondary sector, comprehensive education and the content of the school curriculum. In this respect, much research and writing in the sociology of education has paralleled the developments that have taken place in the educational system. As a result, much sociological work has been preoccupied with patterns, processes and procedures associated with the system of compulsory schooling. However, we might ask what the main perspectives have been that sociologists have used in their studies.

Recent reviews of the sociology of education in England have tended to draw distinctions between the 'old' or 'traditional' sociology of education and the 'new' sociology of education. Much work in the 1950s and 1960s, with its interest in the relationship between education and the economy, education and social class and patterns of social mobility, has been characterised as the 'traditional' perspective. Meanwhile, the 1970s are said to have heralded the 'new' sociology of education with its emphasis upon schools, classrooms and curricula and questions about the content of education. Such distinctions are very simple and we should be careful about allocating sociological work to the 'old' or 'new' approach. However, it is important to take note of the *perspectives* that are used by sociologists and the way in which these influence the questions that are posed. At the same time, it is essential to focus on the relationship between problems, theories and methods, especially where different perspectives and different methods of social inquiry have been used to investigate the same educational problem, as the evidence that is produced may be very different. It is at this point that debate, dialogue and controversy enter on the scene and readers are required to evaluate the evidence that is made available.

Within the sociology of education many different theoretical perspectives have influenced empirical studies. In the 1950s *structural-functionalism* was a dominant influence in sociology

1

and the sociology of education. From this perspective, educational institutions were seen in terms of their purpose which, it was assumed, was to contribute to the smooth running of society. Sociologists who used this approach concentrated on the structure of educational organisations and the extent to which they achieved certain goals. Schools were, therefore, seen as an important training ground for the young. Such an approach has been the subject of considerable criticism and has been challenged by a number of other approaches.

In contrast to this perspective is *conflict theory* which focuses upon competing interests among individuals and groups. Sociologists who have used this approach have looked at power and control in education and have examined the role of mass education in controlling entrance to the labour market and to higher education through selective mechanisms. In this respect, the focus of interest is very similar to some of the problems that are studied by functionalists, but the explanations that are provided are very different.

A further approach that has had a considerable impact on educational studies in recent years is *interactionism*. This approach is concerned with the patterns and processes of interaction that occur between groups and individuals and the social meanings that are assigned to social situations. Sociologists of education have used this approach to focus on patterns of interaction in schools and classrooms, between teachers and pupils and among pupils. In this respect, the emphasis has been placed upon microscopic as opposed to macroscopic questions that have been posed by other approaches. The empirical studies that sociologists have conducted from this perspective have involved an ethnographic approach based on participant observation, unstructured interviews and documentary evidence rather than large-scale social surveys that have dominated other approaches.

However, it is not just theoretical approaches that have influenced the perspectives that sociologists have taken. The social and political movements of the period have also had some impact upon sociological study. In particular, the women's movement has had a considerable influence upon the shape of sociology since the early 1970s, especially in terms of the questions, concepts and categories that are used in the course of sociological analysis. As a consequence, much sociological writing in education is now concerned with the educational experiences of girls as well as boys and the ways in which the gender concept can be used to focus on areas of educational activity which were previously unquestioned. Such an approach should alert us to consider not only those areas in which sociologists have posed questions and provided explanations, but also to examine the gaps that exist in our knowledge. For example, in the sociology of education it is important to take into account the different educational experience of those individuals from different social class backgrounds and different ethnic groups, as well as comparing the education available for girls and boys.

However, educational experiences have to be set in a broader context and it is this issue that has influenced the arrangement of the chapters in this book. We begin by focusing on key concepts by looking at the meaning of education, socialisation and schooling in the first chapter, which draws on comparative and historical material to highlight the different interpretations associated with education and schooling. A major question that readers should keep in mind is: how is education defined, by whom and for what purpose?

The second chapter turns to education, the economy and the labour market; a field of study which has involved considerable debate and controversy from those working within different theoretical perspectives. Among the questions that sociologists have discussed are: is there a relationship between education and the economy? Is there a relationship between education and industrialisation? In addressing these questions we should be aware that within this field, functionalists and Marxists have examined the relationship between education, the economy and the contemporary labour market. Accordingly, it is the reader's task to consider how to interpret the evidence that different sociologists have advanced as it provides a background to questions of equality and inequality in the next three chapters.

In the course of examining social inequality in the educational system we begin by looking at education and the structure of opportunity. In considering the contributions on concepts and categories concerning equality of educational opportunity and patterns of social mobility, the following questions need to be kept in mind: is there equality of opportunity within education? Does education promote social mobility? Does education reproduce the class structure? Chapter 3 attempts to summarise the key areas of controversy which provide a background to questions about the social processes of educational achievement. Here, sociologists have contributed to the debate on the role of education in patterns of achievement. In particular, this chapter focuses on social factors beyond schools which, it has been argued, have an influence upon educational achievement. Among the main factors considered are: social class, cultural capital, language, gender and race. Here sociologists have to assess the relative importance of each of these factors, especially in relation to those social processes that contribute to success and failure in schools. While Chapters 3 and 4 contribute to separate areas of sociological analysis, they are also linked together in terms of their wide-ranging contribution to the debate about patterns of inequality in education, a theme that recurs in Chapter 5 which focuses on schools.

Sociologists have made a number of contributions to the debate about the process of schooling and the influence of school organisation on the process of education, both of which are discussed in Chapter 5. This theme is also picked up in Chapter 6, where the focus is upon the classroom and the way in which classroom processes involve strategies, negotiations and bargains between teachers and taught. The activities that occur in schools and classrooms provide a background to Chapter 7, which examines the school curriculum and issues concerning social control. Among the questions that are considered are: what is the curriculum? Who determines the curriculum content?

In the course of considering who controls the curriculum and who selects curriculum knowledge, sociologists have asked further questions about politics and decision-making in education. It is this area that is examined in the final chapter which attempts to pick up political and policy-related issues in education in relation to some of the themes that have been examined in earlier chapters. In this way, it is hoped that readers will be encouraged to consider ways in which further themes may be explored by linking together contributions from a number of chapters on such issues as patterns of inequality in education, and class, gender and race, in relation to education.

In this book readers are encouraged not only to consider those questions that relate to the sociology of education but also to fundamental problems about theories and methods in sociology. Among the key issues that readers should consider are: what kinds of questions are posed by the sociologist? What concepts are used? What methods of investigation are used in the collection of empirical data? What explanations are provided? Which concepts, categories and explanations are emphasised and which are neglected? It is by considering such questions that readers will get some taste of the central issues involved in the sociology of education.

FURTHER READING

This introduction has only briefly touched upon some of the main issues and trends in the sociology of education in relation to the content of this book. For readers who wish to obtain more detailed overviews of the main debates, issues and perspectives in this field, the following are recommended:

1. S. Acker, 'No-woman's land: British sociology of education 1960–1979', *Sociological Review*, vol. 29, no. 1 (1981) 77–104.

   A review of the sub-discipline from a feminist perspective. Very useful in challenging assumptions and stereotypes. This article is also in B. Cosin and M. Hales (eds), *Education, Policy and Society*, Routledge and Kegan Paul, 1983, pp. 106–28

2. O. Bank, 'Sociology of education' in L. Cohen, J. Thomas and L. Manion (eds), *Educational Research and Development in Britain 1970–1980*, NFER-Nelson, 1982, pp. 43–54.

   Contains a good synthesis of the major developments and debates.

3. G. Bernbaum, *Knowledge and Ideology in the Sociology of Education*, Macmillan, 1977.

   A short review of the field that is particularly good in distinguishing key features in the 'old' and 'new' sociologies of education.

4. R. G. Burgess, 'Exploring frontiers and settling territory: shaping the sociology of education', *British Journal of Sociology*, vol. 35, no. 1 (1984) 122–37.

   Reviews a range of studies in the early 1980s drawing special attention to the way in which the field of study is defined.

5. R. G. Burgess, *The Sociology of Education*, Batsford, 1986.

   Discusses the major issues in the sociology of education using case study material. It can be used to complement this book.

6. B. Davies, 'The sociology of education', in P. H. Hirst (ed), *Educational Theory and its Foundation Disciplines*, Routledge and Kegan Paul, 1983, pp. 100–45.

   Provides a discussion of sociology alongside other essays that consider those disciplines which relate to educational theory.

7. A. Hartnett (ed), *The Social Sciences in Educational Studies*, Heinemann, 1982.

   A series of bibliographic essays that mainly focus on different areas in the sociology of education. It is well worth consulting to identify major themes and related reading.

8. J. Karabel and A. H. Halsey, 'Introduction', in J. Karabel and A. H. Halsey (eds), *Power and Ideology in Education*, Oxford University Press, 1977, pp. 1–85.

   Reviews major theoretical and methodological issues in the sociology of education.

9. P. Robinson, *Perspectives on the Sociology of Education*, Routledge and Kegan Paul, 1981.

   A useful review of the field that examines theoretical perspectives. It includes a useful chapter on the Third World.

10. P. Woods, *Sociology of the School: An Interactionist Viewpoint*, Routledge and Kegan Paul, 1983.

    A useful synthesis of recent work on schools and classrooms from an interactionist perspective. It is clearly written.

1
Education, socialisation and schooling

It has been calculated that pupils spend 15,000 hours in schools during the period of their compulsory education. Such a statement contains a number of issues that can be questioned by sociologists. First, what is education? Secondly, does eduction equal formal schooling? Thirdly, what activities occur within the 15,000 hours of schooling? It is to some of these issues that we turn in this chapter, as it is all too easy for those of us who are participants in the English educational system to feel that our familiarity with schools and schooling means that we know all about education. Many of our ideas about education and schooling are based on a narrow range of experiences over a short period of time in a particular educational system in the twentieth century. Accordingly, it is the purpose of this chapter to raise questions about what counts as education and what counts as schooling by drawing on sets of evidence from the nineteenth as well as the twentieth centuries and from countries other than England. The contributions that have been included are therefore designed to raise fundamental questions about education and schooling.

We begin by looking at a statement produced by Emile Durkheim, who attempted to define education when looking at the relationship between sociology and education. Durkheim highlights several important points concerning the study of education. First, we should consider *what* it is we are studying in education; a problem that Durkheim resolved by focusing on the characteristics of the educational system. Secondly, we should consider the time period *when* we are studying education, as what counts as 'education' will vary with the period under study. Thirdly, we must look at *how* education may vary with the social class to which individuals belong and the areas in which they live. By considering these three points, Durkheim highlights how education and educational activities are not the same the world over but vary with social circumstances.

Further conceptual issues are discussed by Kevin Harris. He also focuses on education and in turn picks up the concepts 'schooling' and 'socialisation'. Automatically, this raises a number of questions: does education equal schooling? Is education little more than socialisation? Drawing on evidence from different theoretical perspectives, Harris discusses the relationship between education and socialisation. The different ideas and different perspectives that are taken by individuals in the course of discussing education have been classified by Raymond Williams into four broad ideologies. He relates the social position of the individual both to the ideology that is held and the policies that they generate. While this is a useful classification to keep in mind, it does not imply that a particular ideology automatically relates to a social position. It is, therefore, essential to evaluate the ideas that are being presented about education, by whom and for what purpose, in different sets of social circumstances.

If we turn to historical and comparative studies, we find that different sets of ideas are advanced from those with which we are familiar in twentieth-century Britain. However, we need to examine what kinds of activities are being promoted as 'education'. We turn first to a set of rules from a church day school for girls in Cambridgeshire in 1880. These rules include ideas about education, about socialisation and the kind of education that is considered to be appropriate for girls. Following this reading, Williamson's discussion of education in Tanzania brings a comparative perspective to our work by considering questions about the social purposes of education. He looks at the ideas of Julius Nyerere who provided a critique of the educational system in Tanzania and suggested ways in which schools might respond to the demands of that society. This material brings us back to considering the definition of education, the process of socialisation and the use of ideology in shaping a view of education. However, Julius Nyerere's ideas about education take us away from the conventional conception of a school; a theme that is discussed in the remaining extracts in this chapter.

Brian Jackson's focus is upon English schools, but he poses the questions: what is involved in schooling? What messages are learned in the school? His analysis points to the problems that education and schools present for the poor and the poorest and has much in common with the eight Italian schoolboys from Barbiana who, in the course of discussing their own school, provide a fundamental critique of education and of schooling. It is on the basis of such critiques, which argue that schools have failed and do not do what they pretend to do, that writers such as Ivan Illich, Everett Reimer and Paul Goodman have suggested that the school as an institution should be dismantled and replaced by a series of learning networks.

This chapter, therefore, considers some of the ways in which education has been defined by different writers and alerts us to the fact that there are many different kinds of education that can be the subject of sociological study in our own and other societies, in the past as well as in the present.

A DEFINITION OF EDUCATION

Among sociological theorists it is the French sociologist Emile Durkheim who made the most significant contribution to the study of education. His most important works in this field are his published lectures entitled *Education and Sociology*, *Moral Education* and *The Evolution of Educational Thought*. In the former, Durkheim attempts to define education in terms of the characteristics of educational systems.

Reading 1

To define education we must, then, consider, educational systems, present and past, put them together, and abstract the characteristics which are common to them. These characteristics will constitute the definition that we seek.

We have already determined, along the way, two elements. In order that there be education, there must be a generation of adults and one of youth, in interaction, and an influence exercised by the first on the second. It remains for us to define the nature of this influence.

There is, so to speak, no society in which the system of education does not present a twofold aspect: it is at the same time one and manifold.

It is manifold. Indeed, in one sense, it can be said that there are as many different kinds of education as there are different milieux in a given society. Is such a society formed of castes? Education varies from one caste to another; that of the patricians was not that of the plebeians; that of the Brahman was not that of the Sudra. Similarly, in the Middle Ages, what a difference between the culture that the young page received, instructed in all the arts of chivalry, and that of the villein, who learned in his parish school a smattering of arithmetic, song and grammar! Even today, do we not see education vary with social class, or even with locality? That of the city is not that of the country, that of the middle class is not that of the worker. Would one say that this organization is not morally justifiable, that one can see in it only a survival destined to disappear? This proposition is easy to defend. It is evident that the education of our children should not depend upon the chance of their having been born here or there, of some parents rather than others. But even though the moral conscience of our time would have received, on this point, the satisfaction that it expects, education would not, for all that, become more uniform. Even though the career of each child would, in large part, no longer be predetermined by a blind heredity, occupational specialization would not fail to result in a great pedagogical [teaching] diversity. Each occupation, indeed, constitutes a milieu *sui generis* which requires particular aptitudes and specialized knowledge, in which certain ideas, certain practices, certain modes of viewing things, prevail; and as the child must be prepared for the function that he will be called upon to fulfill, education, beyond a certain age, can no longer remain the same for all those to whom it applies. That is why we see it, in all civilized countries, tending more and more to become diversified and specialized; and this specialization becomes more advanced daily. The heterogeneity which is thus created does not rest, as does that which we were just discussing, on unjust inequalities; but it is not less. To find an absolutely homogeneous and egalitarian education, it would be necessary to go back to prehistoric societies, in the structure of which there is no differentiation; and yet these kinds of societies represent hardly more than one logical stage in the history of humanity.

    E. Durkheim, *Education and Sociology*, 1956, pp. 67–9.

Questions
1. *What are the main characteristics that Durkheim associates with education?*
2. *Durkheim states 'In order that there be education, there must be a generation of adults and one of youth in interaction, and an influence exercised by the first on the second.' Do you agree?*
3. *Does Durkheim's definition of education imply socialisation? Give reasons for your answer.*

SCHOOLING AND EDUCATION

Writing from a Marxist perspective, Kevin Harris provides a radical critique of the school system. His principal argument is that teachers educate as agents of socialisation but fail to educate in terms of going beyond socialisation. In the course of the discussion he outlines his views on education, schooling and socialisation.

Reading 2
Teachers, or at least the teachers this [reading] is concerned with,

work in schools. Now what goes on in schools is, at a basic operational level of definition, *schooling*. In our ordinary, everyday language, however, we tend to refer to what goes on in schools as *education*; so much so that the two terms tend to be taken as synonymous or coextensive. We speak of going to school to get an education; the level of people's education is commonly measured by or equated with the number of years they have attended school and the awards gained there; schools themselves are generally categorised and described in terms of being part of the education system; and schools of course come under the control and auspices of education departments, local education authorities, and ministers of education. The school/education nexus is an extremely strong one; so strong in fact that the equivalence of 'schooling' and 'education' is largely taken for granted.

When we consider conjunctions which have come to be taken for granted, or as part of 'the way things are', we often find that both the strength and the tenuousness of the nexus become more clearly revealed by the effect brought about when the nexus is deliberately broken. This is particularly so with regard to the schooling/education nexus. George Bernard Shaw complained that his education was interrupted by his schooling; and Margaret Mead has noted that her grandmother wanted her to have a good education and so kept her out of school. These statements emerge as credible and startling. Their credibility lies in the fact that they were made by people generally considered to be highly Educated; they are startling because they turn on the paradox that schooling is antagonistic to, rather than compatible with, Education. The statements entail far more than a begrudging notion which any of us might make about 'not getting much of an education at school' – they point to a distinct incompatibility between the institution of schooling and the notion of Education; an incompatibility so surprising on first contact that the actual statements themselves have achieved the status of modern epigrams, and tend to appear regularly on desk calendars, as epigraphs to books and articles, and among lists of 'quotable quotes'.

Now there are really two points at issue here; points which actually concern different sides of the same coin. First, there is the problem of the very conflation [fusion or blending together] of 'schooling' and 'education', and turning with this is the issue of which particular sense of 'education' is being conflated with 'schooling'. Consider carefully the following two statements. The first is by Herbert Gintis, and has been extracted from a broadly Marxist context.

> The function of education in any society is the *socialisation* of youth into the prevailing culture. On the one hand, schooling serves to integrate individuals into society by institutionalising dominant value, norm and belief systems. On the other hand, schooling provides the individual competencies necessary for the adequate performance of social roles. Thus education systems are fundamental to the stability and functioning of any society.

The second is by I.L. Kandel, a liberal conservative, commonly charged with being an essentialist:

> The earliest and most persistent reason for the establishment of schools as formal agencies of education is the desire on the part of a group, society, or state to conserve and transmit its cultural heritage to the younger generation and to equip this generation with those habits, skills, knowledges and ideals that will enable it to take its place in a society and contribute to the stability and perpetuation of that society.

There are three things there deserving of particular note. First, although they are speaking from quite different and opposed contexts, both Gintis and Kandel spell out the same message – that the function of education is conservative, being directed towards integrating new generations into the prevailing culture, and providing knowledge and skills geared towards ensuring social stability and perpetuation of the status quo. Second, both authors use the words 'schooling' and 'education' interchangeably (and in doing so they are anything but unusual or exceptional). Third, it is abundantly clear that what they are really talking about is socialisation: the point both authors are making is that schooling is basically a socialising agency or institution.

K. Harris, *Teachers and Classes: A Marxist Analysis*, 1982, pp. 7–8.

Questions
1. *Are 'education' and 'schooling' synonymous (para. 1)?*
2. *George Bernard Shaw claimed that schooling interrupted 'education'. Do you agree?*

3. *What do you understand by 'socialisation'? Are schools agents of socialisation (para. 4)?*
4. *Compare and contrast the major elements involved in your school and non-school education.*

EDUCATIONAL IDEOLOGIES

It is apparent from any review of educational events that different stances are taken towards education by different groups. It is common for all groups to employ ideologies that give a particular emphasis to a perspective or an idea. The relationship between ideology, social position and educational policy is outlined as follows:

Reading 3

Raymond Williams has distinguished four sets of educational philosophies or ideologies which rationalise different emphases in the selection of the content of curricula. He relates these to the social position of those who hold them. Also he suggests that curricula changes have reflected the relative power positions of the different groups over the last hundred years.

Ideology	Social position	Educational policies
1. Liberal/ Conservative	Aristocracy/ gentry	Non-vocational – the 'educated man', an emphasis on character
2. Bourgeois	Merchant and professional classes	Higher vocational and professional courses. Education as access to desired positions
3. Democratic	Radical reformers	Expansionist – 'education for all'
4. Populist/ proletarian	Working classes subordinate groups	Student relevance, choice, participation

J. Evetts, *The Sociology of Educational Ideas*, 1973, p. 123.

Questions

1. *What do you understand by the term 'ideology'?*
2. *Do you share Raymond Williams's view that there is a relationship between ideology, social position and educational policy? Give reasons for your answer.*
3. *Discuss the ways in which different ideologies have influenced English education in the last thirty years.*

EDUCATION IN A NINETEENTH-CENTURY NATIONAL SCHOOL IN ENGLAND

The way in which education has been defined in different ways in different schools at different periods of time is apparent from a study of educational documents. The following rules from a Cambridgeshire Church School for girls in 1880 gives some clues to ideas that were held about education, schooling and socialisation.

Reading 4

R U L E S

OF THE

HASLINGFIELD
NATIONAL SCHOOL

GIRLS.

1. The Children must be sent to School with their hands and faces well washed, and their hair combed and brushed, clothes clean and neat, and they are not allowed to come to School wearing ornaments, feathers, artificials, or any unnecessary article of dress.

2. The School is opened in the morning with prayers, immediately after the Church clock strikes Nine, by which time all the children must be in School and remain till Twelve o'clock; in the afternoon the Children must be in the School by the time that the Church clock strikes Two, and remain, throughout the

year, till Half-past Four o'clock, when the School is closed by prayers.

3. Children of Labourers pay One Penny weekly; Trades-people's Children, Twopence; and the Children of Farmers and other Parishes, Threepence.

4. Girls are admitted into the School at Seven years of age, and *no Child* is admitted under that age, nor till the Trustees are satisfied that any arrears have been paid which may be due to the Infant Schoolmistress. The admissions from the Infant School take place Quarterly.

5. The Mistress is required to keep a register of the attendance of each Child, and also the amount paid weekly by each Child.

6. Any Child coming to School late, who is inattentive, disorderly, or guilty of using bad language, destroying the Property of the School, or otherwise misconducting herself, will be punished by the Mistress at the discretion of the Trustees, and is liable to be discharged from the School.

7. If any of the Parents or Friends of the Children interfere in the regulations made to maintain discipline, and enforce obedience to the Mistress or others in authority, the Children of such persons cannot be allowed to remain in the School.

8. The Mistress is required, in secular instruction, to teach the Girls Reading, Writing, Spelling, English Grammar, Tables, Arithmetic, General History, and Geography, and such subjects of useful knowledge as may from time to time be directed or authorised by the Trustees; in Religious Instruction, Bible Reading and Bible History, the Catechism, Articles of the Church of England, and general knowledge of the Liturgy.

9. The Mistress is required to teach the Girls every kind of plain Needlework, Marking, Stocking and Plain Knitting, Stocking Darning, &c, &c.

10. The Children are allowed to work one week in four for their Parents, but no Child is allowed to bring to the School, under any pretence, any description of Fancy Work, and during the other three weeks, *all the Children* will do any Work, not Fancy work, which can be procured. The afternoon only of each day is allowed for Needlework.

11. Any sum that may be received for work done at the School will be appropriated for the benefit of the Children.

12. The Children are required to attend the Sunday Schools and also Divine Service at the Parish Church, and the Mistress is required to attend and teach the Children on the Sunday morning from Half-past Nine to a Quarter before Eleven, and in the afternoon from Two till a Quarter before Three, and also to superintend their behaviour during Divine Service at Church.

13. One week's holiday is allowed at Christmas, and five weeks at Harvest, and Saturday in every week.

14. Annual Prizes are given to those Boys and Girls under 14 years of age who show on Examination the greatest proficiency in the repetition and general knowledge of the Church Catechism; and to those Children under 15 years who show the like proficiency in the Articles of the Church of England.

15. The Mistress and Teachers are required, so far as is practicable, to set the Children an example in dress; and all the above Rules, where practicable, are to be applied to the Sunday School.

16. The School is subject to the visitation and inspection of Her Majesty's Inspectors of Schools, and of the Diocesan Inspector, and the National Society's Inspector.

17. Any of the above Rules, where practicable, are to be applied to the Sunday School.

P. Gordon and D. Lawton, *Curriculum Change in the Nineteenth and Twentieth Centuries*, 1978, p. 129.

Questions
1. *How do these rules define education for girls?*
2. *Discuss the extent to which these rules point to gender socialisation through the school curriculum.*
3. *Outline the strengths and weaknesses of using this document to provide a sociological analysis of schooling in a church day school in 1880. What other documents would you wish to examine?*

EDUCATION IN TANZANIA

In recent years sociologists have focused their attention on comparative and historical studies in education in order to assess the contribution that education can make to countries in the Third World. In this reading, Bill Williamson examines the ideas of Julius Nyerere on education in Tanzania.

Reading 5

Specifically in the field of education considerable parental dissatisfaction over the failure of primary school graduates to gain secondary school places resulted in demonstrations throughout [Tanzania] in which many education officers were besieged by angry parents demanding school places for their children. In the field of higher education the reluctance of students to take part in the National Service campaign, a reluctance which led the President to dismiss some 300 students from the University, forced into the open the issue of elitist attitudes in Tanzanian education.

Julius Nyerere had been aware of what he understood as a mass-elite gap a long time before the actual demonstration on 22 October 1967 which led to his action. A year previously he had told students who had been complaining about their living conditions that:

> Every time I come to this campus . . . I think again about our decision to build here . . . Anyone who walks off this campus into the nearby villages or who travels up country . . . will observe the contrast in conditions here and the conditions in which the mass of our people live . . . The purpose of establishing a university is to make it possible for us to change these poverty stricken lives . . . We do not build skyscrapers here so that a very few fortunate individuals can develop their own minds and live in comfort . . . We tax the people to build these places only so that young men and women may become efficient servants to them. There is no other justification for this heavy call being made on poor peasants.

And later, while talking to members of the student delegation which accompanied the demonstration against students being involved in national service, the President angrily underlined the point that the political elite and the educated elite were 'members of the same class – the exploiting class'. He went on:

> The man who gets the minimum wage and the poor peasant, they are the ones who have to pay these [i.e. the wages of high salary earner – B.W.] Everybody in this country is paid too much except the poor peasant.

The students had convinced the President that a reorientation was required in Tanzanian education and that the policy of education for self-reliance set out earlier in the year needed reinforcement and hard work if it were ever to succeed.

The policy itself was clear enough. It is based on a recognition that Tanzania will remain a poor rural society for a long time to come and that education must adapt to these realities. Specifically, a poor society could not go on pouring a large proportion of the monetary Gross National Product into a service which has an almost infinite capacity to consume scarce resources and which was clearly not meeting the needs of Tanzanian society. Nyerere detected four main weaknesses in the educational system: it was elitist; it divorced children from the world in which they would eventually have to live; it fostered a respect for book-learning only thereby despising the knowledge of people themselves; finally, it removed young people from direct productive work.

From this analysis Nyerere drew three main policy conclusions. Behind each one is the politically difficult conviction that the problem of primary school leavers could not be solved by expanding secondary school places; something different had to be attempted. Firstly, primary education needed to be a complete education without any implied promise of secondary education and modern sector employment. This implied relating education to rural life and for those few necessary for the economy who require secondary or further education, such education must be seen as helping the people as a whole and not just the individual. Secondly, schools must become communities themselves to give people the skills to live co-operatively. Nyerere argued that every school should become a farm and, where possible, should aim at self-sufficiency. Finally, the curriculum of schools should reflect the needs of peasant communities and give students themselves the skills they need to earn their own living in an egalitarian, socialist society. One component of this is a positive commitment to non-formal education. In Nyerere's analysis the problems of Tanzanian education are clearly linked up to the colonial heritage and the need to overcome that heritage in a disciplined programme of political socialisation and social reform. It is just at this point, however, that his critics have questioned the viability of his plans.

B. Williamson, *Education, Social Structure and Development*, 1979, pp. 161–3.

Questions
1. *How did Nyerere define 'education' in Tanzania?*

2. *What ideas does Nyerere associate with schools and 'schooling' in Tanzania?*
3. *Examine the extent to which education in Tanzania appears to be similar to or different from English education at the present time.*

THE MESSAGES OF SCHOOLING

Schools carry numerous messages, of which some are communicated openly while others are hidden and demand decoding. Brian Jackson highlights some of the messages that are transmitted about education in English schools. He concludes with a proposal for education.

Reading 6

All schools carry open *messages* – CSE, GCE, O and A, and so on – to the wide, wide world. But they also transmit secret messages, decoded most easily of all by the poor. Simplest of all to translate is punctuality. School switches on at 9 a.m., switches off at 4 p.m. Miss clocking-in and you're punished; work over and you're a fool. Essentially, a practice ground for factory work, where you may lose 15 minutes' pay (price of an extra helping of chips) if you get up slowly. Next message is: you're stupid. School is full of marks you can't get, exams you can't pass, and knowledge which is not for or about you. Third, you're abnormal. Look at the books they give you. Do they mirror, articulate, narrate, analyse, *your* life. No: they celebrate Janet-and-John land. You are invisible. Fourth: don't start thinking it all through! The Pavlovian dog-bell pings out every 40 minutes, fragmenting thought. Knowledge is dynamic, and schools have to see it is handled harmlessly. Fifth . . . I leave it to you. Spend only a day with a child at school, and you'll see that it is the secret messages that get across. The open messages are often just the fancy wrapping.

This is a wry, perhaps a wrinkled, point of view. And, of course, good teachers are chipping away, all over the rock face. But if our concern is the poor and the poorest, then it is hard to see education as other than a *Pax Scholastica*. A forceful occupation by the armed few of those lush pastures whose earthy roots and springing sap might promise life to the many. That sounds despairing. But not so: it is description; and ten years at the tiller by a minister of education redistributing and reseeding educational power, would sketch out – given other changes in society, too, of course – a far different future. As it stands, though, a good school offers the poor an escape into a little cavern of creativity, an Aladdin's cave of colour, toys, space, tools – for a few hours. But unless we learn to dispense education into the community, and risk handling live knowledge instead of educational blanks, it is hard to see how education for the poor can be anything but a consolatory interlude.

B. Jackson, 'A question of equality' in J. E. C. MacBeath (ed), *A Question of Schooling*, 1976, pp. 21–2.

Questions
1. *What does Jackson's analysis of the messages of schooling suggest about education (para. 1)?*
2. *What messages have been transmitted to you through schooling?*
3. *How do you perceive 'education' in your school or college?*

AN ALTERNATIVE SCHOOL

Although sociologists have advanced a number of criticisms of schools, a most effective message is also transmitted by eight Italian boys at the School of Barbiana which was founded by a Catholic priest in Tuscany. In addressing teachers, the boys raise fundamental questions about schooling and education while discussing the methods adopted in their school.

Reading 7

Compulsory school   After the five elementary years I had the right to three more years of schooling. In fact, the Constitution says that I had the obligation to go. But there was not yet an intermediate school in Vicchio. To go to Borgo was an undertaking. The few who had tried it had spent a pile of money and then were thrown out as failures like dogs.

In any case, the teacher had told my family that it was better not to waste money on me: 'Send him into the fields. He is not made for books.'

My father did not reply. He was thinking, 'If we lived in Barbiana, he *would* be made for books.'

Barbiana In Barbiana all the boys were going to school. The priest's school. From early morning until dark, summer and winter. Nobody there was 'not made for school'.

But we were from a different parish and lived far away. My father was ready to give up. Then he heard of a boy from San Martino who was going to Barbiana. He took courage and went to find out.

The woods When he came back I saw that he had bought me a torch for the dark evenings, a canteen for soup and boots for the snow.

The first day he took me there himself. It took us two hours because we were breaking our path with a sickle and a billhook. Later I learned to make it in little more than an hour.

I would pass by only two houses along the way. Windows broken, recently abandoned. At times I would start running because of a viper or because a crazy man, who lived alone at the Rock, would scream at me from the distance.

I was eleven years old. You would have been scared to death. You see, we each have our different kind of timidity. So, in that sense we are even.

But we're even only if both of us stay at home. Or if you have to come and give us the exams at our place. But you don't have to do that.

The tables Barbiana, when I arrived, did not seem like a school. No teacher, no desk, no blackboard, no benches. Just big tables, around which we studied and also ate.

There was just one copy of each book. The boys would pile up around it. It was hard to notice that one of them was a bit older and was teaching.

The oldest of these teachers was sixteen. The youngest was twelve, and filled me with admiration. I made up my mind from the start that I, too, was going to teach.

The favourite Life was hard up there too. Discipline and squabbles until you didn't feel like coming back.

But there a boy who had no background, who was slow or lazy, was made to feel like the favourite. He would be treated the way you teachers treat the best student in the class. It seemed as if the school was meant just for him. Until he could be made to understand, the others would not continue.

Break   There was no break. Not even Sunday was a holiday.

None of us was bothered by it because labour would have been worse. But any middle-class gentleman who happened to be around would start a fuss on this question.

Once a big professor held forth: 'You have never studied pedagogy, Father Milani. Doctor Polianski writes that sports for boys is a physiopsycho . . .'[1]

He was talking without looking at us. A university professor of education doesn't have to look at schoolboys. He knows them by heart, the way we know our multiplication tables.

Finally he left, and Lucio, who has thirty-six cows in the barn at home, said, 'School will always be better than cow shit.'

The peasants of the world   That sentence can be engraved over the front doors of your schools. Millions of farm boys are ready to subscribe to it. You say that boys hate school and love play. You never asked us peasants. But there are one hundred thousand, nine hundred million of us. Six boys out of every ten in the world feel the same as Lucio. About the other four we can't say.

All your culture is built this way. As if you were all the world.

Children as teachers   The next year I was a teacher; that is, three half-days a week. I taught geography, mathematics and French to the first intermediate year.

You don't need a degree to look through an atlas or explain fractions.

If I made some mistakes, that wasn't so bad. It was a relief for the boys. We would work them out together. The hours would go by quietly, without worry and without fear. You don't know how to run a class the way I do.

Politics or stinginess   Then, too, I was learning so many things while I taught. For instance, that others' problems are like mine. To come out of them together is good politics. To come out alone is stinginess.

I was not vaccinated against stinginess myself. During exams I felt like sending the little ones to hell and studying on my own. I was a boy like your boys, but up at Barbiana I couldn't admit it to myself or to others. I had to be generous even when I didn't feel it.

To you this may seem a small thing. But for your students you

do even less. You don't ask anything of them. You just
encourage them to push ahead on their own.

1. pedagogy: the art of educating children.

Polianski: we never heard this name, but he must be a famous educator.

physiopsycho: the first half of a big word used by that professor, we cannot
remember the ending.

School of Barbiana, *Letter to a Teacher*, 1970, pp. 18–20.

Questions
1. *In what ways is the School of Barbiana different from a conventional
   school?*
2. *What messages are being transmitted about schooling to the pupils at
   Barbiana?*
3. *What sociological concepts would you use to discuss the processes of
   schooling that you have identified at Barbiana?*

DESCHOOLING

Schools and schooling are held by many commentators to be
inappropriate. Ivan Illich is among those who propose a radical
solution for dealing with such educational problems by deschooling; the end of the school and its replacement by patterns of
education that do not depend on institutions. The concept is
examined by Ian Lister.

Reading 8

The concept of *deschooling* presupposes a concept of schooling,
both in theory and practice. Generally speaking, when writers
refer to the 'schooled society' they are talking about the universal
and compulsory systems of education which have developed in
several states during the last two hundred years. They are talking
about the kind of formal education offered by institutions such as
schools, colleges, and universities, as opposed to the informal
and incidental education received from life and experience. Most
of the deschooling writers tend to analyse schools in functional
terms and then create a generalised stereotype of 'the school' or
'schooling'. Much of the argument is in terms of generalisations.
However, there is no school of deschoolers: even in the Mexican
deschooling Mecca of Cuernavaca there are differences in the
thinking of Ivan Illich and Everett Reimer. Thus, the concept of
deschooling can be approached from two other directions – first

to see what the concept is not, and second to see the different use
that different people make of the concept. Extreme criticism of
schools, such as that made in the USA in the nineteenth century
or by Bernard Shaw in his preface to *Misalliance* in 1910, cannot
by itself constitute an argument for deschooling. This is because
deschooling is not merely a negative concept: as used by the
advocates of deschooling it implies a positive programme of
alternatives – alongside the reduction in the role of schools goes
an *expansion* of educational opportunities in order to achieve
lifelong education and the learning society. Paul Goodman
introduced many of the themes of the deschooling argument. He
exposed education as the largest industry of modern society; the
'school-monks' as 'an invested intellectual class worse than
anything since the time of Henry VIII' and argued that if we want
to get education into society we must first get it out of the
schools. He challenged the schools in moral terms: 'The schools
less and less represent any human values, but simply an
adjustment to a mechanical system.' And he challenged the whole
existence of compulsory schooling: 'The belief that a highly
industrialised society requires twelve to twenty years of prior
processing of the young is an illusion or a hoax.' He used
metaphors in his arguments – the school as prison, the school as
concentration camp. He argued for an education which would be
'human' and 'natural' – which he thought school was not. He
argued for a general deinstitutionalisation and deformalisation of
education, and a growth in incidental education – learning by
experience. Decades ago he was writing about the crisis of
community which is behind many of our educational dilemmas.
Most of these things reappear in the writings of Illich and
Reimer. Illich's peculiarity, perhaps, is that as a left-wing
Catholic he argues on a religious level: he talks of 'education or
celebration' and applies the Catholic and Marxist concept of
alienation to schools – 'School makes alienation preparatory to
life, thus depriving education of reality and work of creativity.'
Everett Reimer, whose background is as colourful as, but
different from, that of Illich, speaks of deschooling as being
necessary for our 'secular salvation'. Thus, deschooling is used to
describe a process, or rather a number of allegedly related
processes which culminate in some kind of religious experience.
In brief, deschooling is not a precise concept, with clear
delimitations – and nor would its creators wish it to be. It is less
of a concept than a general drift of thinking. Nor could it be

located within a discipline – such as sociology, psychology, or philosophy: indeed it is one of the greatest strengths of Goodman, Illich and Reimer that – unlike many education thinkers in England – they are not the prisoners of any single discipline.

> I. Lister, 'The concept of deschooling and the future of secondary education' in I. Lister (ed), *Deschooling: A Reader*, 1974, pp. 89–90.

Questions

1. *What do you understand by the concept 'deschooling'?*
2. *Critically evaluate the deschoolers' analysis of schools.*
3. *In what ways do the deschoolers' arguments challenge sociological analyses of education?*

ESSAY QUESTIONS

1. 'Education is a powerful process of socialization, shaping and reinforcing the child's whole self.' Explain what is meant by this definition. Can education determine a child's value, its gender and its ethnicity? (JMB, 1980)

2. Explain and evaluate sociologically the ideas of 'deschooling'. (London, 1982)

3. Discuss the ways in which education contributes to national development making reference to *two* Third World countries.

4. Explain what is meant by 'socialisation' and discuss the use of this concept in the sociological study of education.

FURTHER READING

1. P. Aries, *Centuries of Childhood*, Penguin, 1973 (originally published in 1960).

   A classic that charts the changing concept of childhood. It has a useful index on 'schools' and part two and the conclusion are especially relevant.

2. L. Barton and S. Walker (eds), *Schools, Teachers and Teaching*, Falmer Press, 1982.

   The papers by Bill Williamson (1982) and by June Purvis (1982) are particularly good on the meaning of education in nineteenth-century England.

3. P. Gordon and D. Lawton, *Curriculum Change in the Nineteenth and Twentieth Centuries*, Hodder and Stoughton, 1978.

   A fascinating analysis of curriculum change with case studies of particular subjects.

4. K. Harris, *Teachers and Class: A Marxist Analysis*, Routledge and Kegan Paul, 1982.

A radical approach to education, schooling and the socialisation process.

5. I. Illich, *Deschooling Society*, Penguin, 1973.

The classic critique of schooling. See especially ch. 2.

6. I. Lister, (ed), *Deschooling: A Reader*, Cambridge University Press, 1974.

Contains a range of short papers on deschooling. Well worth consulting.

7. E. Reimer, *School is Dead*, Penguin, 1973.

An analysis of the schooling system from a deschooler.

8. B. Salter and T. Tapper, *Education, Politics and the State*, Grant McIntyre, 1981.

Contains two chapters that discuss educational ideologies especially in relation to English educational events in the 1960s and 1970s.

9. School of Barbiana, *Letter to a Teacher*, Penguin, 1970.

A book by eight Italian schoolboys that raises educational issues which are of direct relevance to sociologists.

10. B. Williamson, *Education, Social Structure and Development*, Macmillan, 1979.

Contains chapters on education in a range of societies using comparative and historical analyses.

2
Education, economy and the labour market

Questions concerning the relationship between education and the economy and education and industry are part of a long-standing debate that has its origins in the nineteenth century and has continued down to the present day. Among the contributors to this debate have been historians, economists, politicians and sociologists who have been engaged in the interpretation and reinterpretation of data in the course of addressing questions that not only focus attention upon the educational system but also on the relationship between school, employment and unemployment. It is, therefore, the purpose of this chapter to include a range of source materials that look not only at the debate about education and industrialisation discussed by Dore, but also at more recent material on education and the labour market in the United Kingdom. As with many areas of sociological investigation, different theoretical perspectives have been used to address broadly similar questions and it is to these perspectives that we now turn.

The dominant theoretical focus in the sociology of education has been functionalism and this has been used to formulate issues and questions on education and the economy. Writing in the 1960s, Halsey, Floud and Anderson (1961) maintained that 'as the economies of the advanced countries are increasingly dominated by scientific and technological innovation, education and the economy become more closely geared, until the educational system occupies a strategic place as a central determinant of the economic, political, social and changing relations of education' (p. 3). A central feature of this perspective is the way in which the educational system becomes essential for economic growth and the development of resources in an industrial society. It is argued that schooling provides each generation with the skills demanded by increased technological and occupational requirements; secondly, that the selective mechanism of schooling helps to allocate individuals to particular jobs; thirdly, that schooling contributes to consensus and to a cohesive society. This approach has been criticised as it has been argued that those who are most qualified are not necessarily the most productive. Furthermore, it is considered that functionalism overestimates the role of technology, underestimates conflict and ideology and ignores the content of education. Yet as the reading from Karabel and Halsey indicates, this approach does focus sociologists' attention on the relationship between education and the economy.

Among the issues that were raised in the late 1950s and early 1960s was the question of whether educational investment was worthwhile. Such a question embraced the notion of educational efficiency and human resources and was addressed by human capital theory. While this perspective can be found in the work of Adam Smith and Alfred Marshall, its revival can be seen in Theodore Schultz's address to the American Economic Association in 1960, where he argued that education was a means of investment through which individuals can enlarge the choices available to them. This idea was taken up in Britain and the USA, especially in relation to the development of higher education (see the reading from Sanderson). Yet some ten years later this approach has been attacked for its failure to tackle poverty and educational inequality, or to promote economic growth in the Third World. It is, therefore, no longer regarded as an adequate framework within which to situate the relationship between education and the economy.

In the 1970s, Marxist and neo-Marxist perspectives attracted a considerable following among sociologists of education. One of the most well-known analyses is that advanced by the American economists Samuel Bowles and Herbert Gintis in their book *Schooling in Capitalist America* (1976). They examined similar issues to the functionalists in their analysis of the relationship between education and the economy. It is their view that industrial capitalism shapes the educational system, for they argue that the hierarchy of authority which is present in the social relations of capitalism is also reflected in the schooling process. This view suggests a degree of correspondence between the educational system and the social division of labour and is therefore concerned with the way in which education is related to the economic organisation of society. It is these views that have been the subject of considerable debate by commentators such as Karabel and Halsey (1977) and Musgrove (1979) among many others. Although commentators have highlighted some of the similarities that exist between functionalism and correspondence theory, they also raise questions about the extent to which Bowles and Gintis's views are mechanistic, deterministic and applicable to Britain.

It is this question of the applicability of theoretical perspectives to the relationship between education and the economy that is taken up in the last four readings in this chapter. In the 1960s it was assumed that educational expansion contributed to economic growth, but by the 1970s the dominant view was that education inhibited the growth of industry. It is against this background that Dan Finn and Simon Frith examine the relationships between schooling and the labour market in Britain in the 1960s and

1970s. Their analysis provides clues to the ways in which sociologists might interpret the developments that have occurred in the schools and the programmes that have been developed by the Manpower Services Commission.

How, we might ask, do boys and girls respond to the transition between school and the labour market in the 1970s and 1980s? The accounts by Paul Willis, who focuses on boys in the West Midlands, and by Helen Roberts, who looks at girls in Bradford, help us to address questions about the relationship between education, the economy and the labour market. Finally, the data provided by Brian Main and David Raffe link up with the debate about education and unemployment (cf. Watts, 1983) by looking at the relationship between education and labour market status among a sample of school-leavers in Scotland.

On this basis, the readings provided in this chapter consider historical and contemporary data using theoretical and empirical materials. As we shall see, the writers' views are shaped in part by the context in which they are writing, the evidence that they use and the theoretical framework that is established. However, at the heart of all these discussions is the relationship between education and industry which provides a backdrop against which patterns of educational opportunity and social inequality can be considered in subsequent chapters.

EDUCATION AND INDUSTRIALISATION

The relationship between education and industrialisation has been the subject of continued debate among those sociologists and historians who have considered whether economic growth was a cause of educational expansion. Ronald Dore provides a summary of the key phases in English education in relation to the process of industrialisation. While he argues that economic expansion was not a consequence of education, he is careful not to overstate his case.

Reading 1

It would be hard to make out a case for believing that the economic growth of Britain was a consequence of improved or expanded education.

> The industrial revolution was accomplished by hard heads and clever fingers. Men like Bramah and Maudslay, Arkwright and Crompton, the Darbys of Coalbrookdale and Neilson of Glasgow, had no systematic education in science and technology. Britain's industrial strength lay in its amateurs and self-made men: the craftsman-inventor, the

mill-owner, the iron-master . . . In this rise of British industry the British universities played no part; indeed formal education of any sort was a negligible factor in its success. The schools attended scarcely changed since the schooldays of John Milton two centuries earlier. For the working classes there was no systematic schooling. Illiteracy was widespread: even as late as 1841 a third of the men and nearly half the women who were married in England and Wales signed the register with a mark. (Ashby, 1961, p. 466.)

One can, to be sure, overstress this point. The basic general education which some of the entrepreneurs and inventors of the late eighteenth and early nineteenth centuries received was probably not irrelevant to their later careers. Significantly a higher proportion of them were former pupils of the dissenting academies than can be explained by mere chance . . . which, given the state of the public schools patronised by the orthodox Anglican gentry, is perhaps not surprising.

There are also reasonable grounds for saying that the *relevant* statistic is that two-thirds of the men *could* write their names when they got married, rather than that one-third couldn't. Anderson's '40% threshold', his thesis that for all the major historical cases of economic growth an overall 40 per cent school enrolment rate seems to have been a precondition . . . has a certain plausibility. Economic growth in Britain was not just a matter of a few inventions in the textile industry and in engineering; it depended on numerous rationalising initiatives of farmers and merchants and craftsmen and small entrepreneurs. And eighteenth-century Britain did have institutionalised means of teaching enough of the young to read and write and calculate – even, sometimes, to think – to provide a sizeable number of men capable of such initiatives.

But – to summarise the argument of the following brief and perhaps idiosyncratic (but at least purposefully so) history of British education:

1. There was no spurt in educational provision preceding or accompanying the acceleration of economic growth known as the industrial revolution.

2. The effect of early *industrialisation* was, if anything, to harden the divisions between the schools of different social strata, rather than to provide channels for social mobility.

3. It was not until industrialisation was well under way that the state began to play a role of any importance in the direction of the educational system.

4. It took even longer before the state's management of the educational system became much affected by the intention to stimulate or sustain economic growth – to meet national training needs, etc.

5. And it was even later still that the national training needs were seen to require the 'sponsored mobility' of bright children from the poorer classes through the educational system to man the expanding middle-class occupations.

6. Meanwhile, until this happened, the occupation of a man depended chiefly on family connections which secured entry into different kinds of craft and professional apprenticeships, and on his ability to develop the necessary competence during his apprenticeship, and afterwards on the job. It also depended in part on what he had *learned* in school, but not much on any certificates or qualifications he might have got from school.

7. The standards of competence required by various crafts and professions gradually became more precisely defined – at first by the practitioners who established their own means of testing and certifying skills.

8. But gradually public authorities took an increasing hand in the definition of competence, beginning with the professions of most direct public concern such as medicine.

9. And (as a related, but not identical trend) general educational qualifications granted by the core educational system of elementary and secondary schools, colleges and universities, have played an increasing role in the control over access to occupations.

10. With the result that *the social definition of the purpose of schooling* has changed and with it the motivation of students and the quality of learning.

> R. Dore, *The Diploma Disease: Education, Qualification and Development*, 1976, pp. 14–15.

Questions
1. *What do you understand by 'industrialisation'?*
2. *Summarise Dore's arguments concerning the relationship between education and industrialisation.*
3. *Outline and discuss alternative arguments to Dore's on the relationship between education and industrialisation.*

4. *In what ways has 'the social definition of the purpose of schooling'
changed in England in the last 100 years?*

A FUNCTIONALIST ACCOUNT

The functionalist perspective maintains that education is an
important precondition for economic growth. It is argued that
with industrialisation the educational system fulfils particular
needs by performing various functions on behalf of society.
Karabel and Halsey set this perspective in context and outline
some of its key features.

Reading 2

After the Second World War, the United States and the Soviet
Union became engaged in a 'cold war,' a crucial component of
which was the 'battle of production.' Could the Western powers,
emerging from the dislocations of depression and war, surpass
the impressive material and technological progress of their Soviet
rival? The development of nuclear weapons had provided
dramatic evidence that technological superiority could be con-
verted into military dominance. Both countries therefore looked
to their systems of education to produce an adequate flow of
scientists and engineers, and this added to the traditional concern
with 'human resources,' which, at least in America, dated from
the Depression. In 1949, the four major American national
research councils appointed a Commission on Human Resources
and Advanced Training. The Commission, directed by Dael
Wolfle, sponsored a widely influential study, *America's Resources
of Specialized Talent*, which appeared in 1954. In a statement
characteristic of the period, Wolfle warned that 'survival itself
may depend on making the most effective use of the nation's
intellectual resources'. Later but similarly in Britain, the Robbins
Report on Higher Education, which appeared in 1963, was at
pains to stress the importance of educating potential talent and to
attack traditionally entrenched conceptions of a limited pool of
educable ability.

This concern with the preservation of human resources marked
the particular variety of functionalist theory that was most
popular in educational research in the 1950s. Thus Burton Clark,
a prominent contributor to the sociology of education in
America, in 1962 published a textbook under the title *Educating*

the Expert Society in which he put forward a lucid version of what might be called technological *functionalism*. Emphasizing the rapidity of technological change, Clark declared that, 'our age demands army upon army of skilled technicians and professional experts, and to the task of preparing these men the educational system is increasingly dedicated'. Seen in this light, the expansion and the increasing differentiation of the educational system were inevitable outcomes of technologically determined changes in occupational structure requiring ever more intricate skills. At the same time, the drive for educational efficiency was congruent with the traditional socialist critique of inequality of educational opportunity between classes. At the level of policy Clark's functional analysis supported a program of transformation of the schools both to promote equal opportunity at home and to turn back 'the expanding thrust of totalitarianism abroad'.

Clark's formulation seems in retrospect to reflect some of the underlying ideological components of the technological functionalism which became fashionable after Russia launched Sputnik in 1957.

> Greater schooling for greater numbers also *has brought with it* and *evidently implies*, a greater practicality in what the schools teach and what they do for students. The existence of children of diverse ability *calls forth* the comprehensive school, or the multischool comprehensive structure, within which some students receive a broad general education but others take primarily a technical or commercial training. In short, increased quantity *means* greater vocationalism . . . Sorting *must* take place at some point in the education structure. If, at that level, it does not take place at the door, it *must* occur inside the doors, in the classroom and counseling office . . .
>
> Democracy encourages aspiration, and generous admission allows the student to carry his hopes into the school or now principally the college. But there his desires run into the standards *necessary* for the integrity of programs and the training of competent workers. The college offers the opportunity to try, but the student's own ability and his accumulative record of performance finally *insist* that he be sorted out . . . (1962:79–80; italics ours)
>
> J. Karabel and A. H. Halsey (eds), *Power and Ideology in Education*, 1977, pp. 8–9.

Questions

1. *What is 'functionalism' (para. 2)? Illustrate the way in which this theory can be applied to education.*

2. *Is there a relationship between technological change and educational change?*

3. *Comment on the statement 'our age demands army upon army of skilled technicians and professional experts, and to the task of preparing these men the educational system is increasingly dedicated' (para. 2). What sociological perspectives have you used in your critique?*

HUMAN CAPITAL THEORY AND UNIVERSITY DEVELOPMENT

Human capital theory was used in the 1960s to justify educational expenditure. Theodore Schultz argued that the labourer could be regarded as an owner of capital who invests in the acquisition of knowledge and skills. Education was seen as a way of improving technological efficiency, increasing productivity and eradicating poverty. In Britain, these ideas were used in arguments concerned with the expansion of higher education in the 1960s which is discussed by Sanderson.

Reading 3

There . . . seemed to be some connections between higher education and economic growth that justified expansion. Since 1945, Britain had experienced relatively slow growth of the Gross Domestic Product of 2·5 per cent per annum compared with Germany's 7·6 and France's 4·6. Britain's was in fact the lowest in Europe. Our 2·4 per cent per annum growth rate for productivity was also the second lowest in Europe. It can be pointed out such comparisons were necessarily vitiated by the destruction of the war and the lower levels from which other European countries began their recoveries. It was also observed that although our growth rates appeared low in comparison with Europe in an unusual period of recovery, yet they were quite normal compared with our own historical experience of growth back to 1900. Yet whatever the qualifications and the realities of the matter, the belief in our laggard slow growth and the need to rectify it became an element in the faith invested in the expansion of higher education at that time. This was one of the implicit assumptions in the Robbins report itself. While denying the possibility of measuring net social gain or of estimating aggregate manpower needs of industry, they considered that there must be a relation between the stock of education and the productivity of industry, and that even though exact rates of return could never be calculated yet external economies must accrue however unquantifiable they may be. The PEP report of 1960 also called for an expansion of scientific education as one of the ways out of slow post-war growth. Firmer data on the connection between high growth rates and levels of higher education in Europe were presented by Michael Kaser in 1963 which gave some plausibility to such views. Comparing percentage per annum growth of Gross National Product and numbers of university students per 1,000 primary students, Kaser found the following relationships for various dates in the 1950s: Japan 7% 48; Germany 11% 41; Sweden 5% 17; Italy 5% 35; France 5% 28. And then at the bottom of the league for growth and next to the bottom for university students came England and Wales 2% 20. Kaser was careful to point out that he was drawing no conclusions about the contribution of higher education to economic growth, indeed the sequence of cause and effect may have been the reverse. But it was not totally naïve at that time for advocates of expansion to believe that one of the contributory ways for Britain to raise her levels of growth to those of her major competitors was for her to raise her levels of higher education to their levels also.

Whatever reservations economists may have felt about the possibility of quantifying such assumptions, British industry itself was clear that it would benefit from the expansion of higher education. Looking back over the scramble for science graduates in the 1940s and 1950s, they were well aware that the universities had not kept pace with the demands of industry and they hoped that an expansion would rectify this by raising university entrance from 4 to 7 per cent of school leavers, providing a 'more prolonged period of broadly based education'. It was noted that 'there is a tremendous amount of goodwill in industry towards these amazing proposals for the development of higher education'.

M. Sanderson, *The Universities and British Industry*, 1972, pp. 362–3.

Questions
1. *What does Sanderson consider to be one of the main assumptions of the Robbins report?*

2. *How would you account for the expansion of scientific education in England?*
3. *What evidence is there to suggest that the development of higher education was a manifestation of human capital theory?*

THE CORRESPONDENCE PRINCIPLE

The 1970s witnessed a growth in the influence of Marxist and neo-Marxist writing about education. In particular, Bowles and Gintis argued that the educational system shapes the consciousness of future workers. Schooling has reproduced the social relations of production through the correspondence between school and class structure and school and industry.

Reading 4

The educational system helps integrate youth into the economic system, we believe, through a structural correspondence between its social relations and those of production. The structure of social relations in education not only inures the student to the discipline of the work place, but develops the types of personal demeanor, modes of self-presentation, self-image, and social-class identifications which are the crucial ingredients of job adequacy. Specifically, the social relationships of education – the relationships between administrators and teachers, teachers and students, students and students, and students and their work – replicate the hierarchical division of labor. Hierarchical relations are reflected in the vertical authority lines from administrators to teachers to students. Alienated labor is reflected in the student's lack of control over his or her education, the *alienation* of the student from the curriculum content, and the motivation of school work through a system of grades and other external rewards rather than the student's integration with either the process (learning) or the outcome (knowledge) of the educational 'production process.' Fragmentation in work is reflected in the institutionalized and often destructive competition among students through continual and ostensibly meritocratic ranking and evaluation. By attuning young people to a set of social relationships similar to those of the work place, schooling attempts to gear the development of personal needs to its requirements.

But the correspondence of schooling with the social relations of production goes beyond this aggregate level. Different levels of education feed workers into different levels within the occupational structure and, correspondingly, tend toward an internal organization comparable to levels in the hierarchical division of labor. As we have seen, the lowest levels in the hierarchy of the enterprise emphasize rule-following, middle levels, dependability, and the capacity to operate without direct and continuous supervision while the higher levels stress the internalization of the norms of the enterprise. Similarly, in education, lower levels (junior and senior high school) tend to severely limit and channel the activities of students. Somewhat higher up the educational ladder, teacher and community colleges allow for more independent activity and less overall supervision. At the top, the elite four-year colleges emphasize social relationships conformable with the higher levels in the production hierarchy. Thus schools continually maintain their hold on students. As they 'master' one type of behavioral regulation, they are either allowed to progress to the next or are channeled into the corresponding level in the hierarchy of production. Even within a single school, the social relationships of different tracks tend to conform to different behavioral norms. Thus in high school, vocational and general tracks emphasize rule-following and close supervision, while the college track tends toward a more open atmosphere emphasizing the internalization of norms.

These differences in the social relationships among and within schools, in part, reflect both the social backgrounds of the student body and their likely future economic positions. Thus blacks and other minorities are concentrated in schools whose repressive, arbitrary, generally chaotic internal order, coercive authority structures, and minimal possibilities for advancement mirror the characteristics of inferior job situations. Similarly, predominantly working-class schools tend to emphasize behavioral control and rule-following, while schools in well-to-do suburbs employ relatively open systems that favor greater student participation, less direct supervision, more student electives, and, in general, a value system, stressing internalized standards of control.

The differential socialization patterns of schools attended by students of different social classes do not arise by accident. Rather, they reflect the fact that the educational objectives and expectations of administrators, teachers, and parents (as well as the responsiveness of students to various patterns of teaching and control) differ for students of different social classes.

S. Bowles and H. Gintis, *Schooling in Capitalist America*, 1976, pp. 131–2.

Questions

1. *Summarise Bowles and Gintis's arguments on the relationship between the school and the workplace.*
2. *What is 'alienation' (para. 1)? How can this concept be used in relation to education?*
3. *Is the correspondence principle relating schooling to the social relations of work applicable to the English educational system? Give reasons for your answer.*

THE LOOSE RELATIONSHIP BETWEEN SCHOOL AND WORK

Dan Finn and Simon Frith focus on the relationship between school and work in England in the 1960s. In particular, they draw attention to the characteristics of this relationship and the way in which it has changed in relation to changing economic circumstances.

Reading 5

Within the schools then the relevance of education to work was defined in a relatively loose way. Even when it was argued that the 'less able' would require a more 'relevant' curriculum, the emphasis was on *education* in opposition to *training*. The Newsom Report, for example, stated that 'such (work-related) courses should be more widely available in all areas'. One of the Report's recommendations was that 'all schools should provide a choice of programme, including a range of courses broadly related to occupational interests, for pupils in the fourth and fifth years of a five year course'. However, the Report was adamant that this vocational element should not exclude other matters: 'Equally, attention should be paid both to the imaginative experience through the arts, and to the personal and social development of the pupils.' Significantly, vocationally biased courses were to be treated as 'vehicles of general education' . . .

Similarly, while the sixties also saw the expansion of the Youth Employment Service, this had only an indirect relationship to the curriculum. Moreover, in the context of a buoyant youth labour market, its emphasis was largely on the career guidance and job placement of young school-leavers.

In the sixties then, the relationship between school and work appeared to be largely unproblematic. The organizational structure of schooling was changed in successive attempts to provide more people, particularly within the working class, with an education which economists, sociologists and politicians regarded, without question, as a 'good' thing. Protected by the argument that more education equals economic growth, the loose and relatively unstructured relationship between school and work seemed to be all that was necessary.

However, with the gradual demise of full employment and the growing numbers of unemployed young people, the question of the transition from school to work was to receive increasing political prominence. Similarly, the accelerating decline of the British economy was to undercut the assumption of an unprob-lematic relationship between educational expansion, in its sixties form, and economic growth. In effect, the sixties witnessed a period of marked autonomy of major sectors of the education system. In the seventies, by contrast, massive *efforts* were made to *ensure a closer conformity between the education system and the necessities of production.*

It is important to grasp the nature of the autonomy which we have used to characterize the schools in the 1960s. We are not suggesting the absence of a relationship to the economy, but on the contrary, we are arguing that the particular political and ideological expression of that relationship involved specific forms of educational reform and expansion, which in turn allowed educational practices to develop in certain ways. It is this pattern of practices and institutional arrangements, particularly in the schools, which was to come under attack in the 1970s.

D. Finn and S. Frith, 'Education and the labour market' in Open University, *The State and the Politics of Education*, 1981, pp. 48–9.

Questions
1. *On what basis would you distinguish between 'education' and 'training' (para. 1)?*
2. *Summarise Finn and Frith's views on the relationship between schooling and the economy in the 1960s.*
3. *What sociological questions would you pose about the relationship between school and work in the 1960s?*

4. *What evidence is there to suggest that the 1970s have witnessed*
   'efforts . . . to ensure a closer conformity between the education system
   and the necessities of production' (para. 4)? What do you think is the
   relationship betwen school and work in the 1980s?

THE TRANSITION FROM SCHOOL FOR
WORKING-CLASS BOYS

Much of the work on education and the economy has been
examined with reference to the educational system. Meanwhile,
Paul Willis looks at this relationship by focusing attention on the
school. His ethnographic study of boys raises questions about
vocational guidance and the status of 'careers' advice and
educational qualifications.

Reading 6

The old *meritocratic model* of the fitting of ability to work profiles
massively persists of course, particularly in the lectures given by
outside speakers. This speaker on the construction industry is
typical:

> We take all kinds of kids, those with CSEs and those
> without, though if you've got CSEs of course, so much the
> better. If you come in at the craft level, you go to college to
> get the City and Guilds . . . that's the first level. Now if
> you've got your craft qualification you can go on . . . if you
> get to the final stage you can become a craft technician . . .
> and if you really want to you can carry on and there's a
> chance of going to Aston University to get a degree . . . So
> you can go as far as you like, and you should go as far as you
> can . . . [in answer to a question from Joey] 'Painting', what
> do you mean by 'painting'? You could learn to paint that
> wall in twenty-four hours, is that what you want? Why not
> think of doing something a bit more, going a bit further on
> than that, say an interior decorator where you have to think
> about your colour design, plan it out, have a job left to you,
> not simply stand there and splash it on . . . We won't stop
> you if you're really keen to get on.*

And inside the school where the main teaching paradigm has
already been *differentiated* with respect to working class values,
and where there is an obvious resistance – or, as is usually
recorded, 'rudeness' – from 'the lads', this careers/counselling

approach can yield to a more abrasive approach. When patience has run out after continuous barracking, or a series of 'let downs', or a patent lack of interest, there is a typical sharp and exclusive re-evaluation of what the teacher stands for, often in the form of a blunt review of the unmodified meritocratic model – bottom end upwards. Despite the 'relevant' personal analogy the following kind of remark has a much older sting.

Careers teacher to fifth year

Some of you think you can just walk in and get an apprenticeship with your standards. Your standards! Some of you can hardly write and read and add up and you think you've got a right to an apprenticeship . . . let me tell you, you have no right at all, not by a long shot, you don't have a right to anything and the sooner you appreciate that, the better you'll do. I haven't the right to expect a good job myself, despite all the training. I don't have the right to a promotion . . . I've got to work towards it, work to deserve it.*

A one-sided, potent and bastardised form of relevance/ progressivism is often resorted to in an attempt to hold the axis of control and pedagogic security. Since relevance is about the return to working class themes, and since working class themes importantly centre on work, there is obviously a temptation to assert attitudes and requirements appropriate to working life retrospectively on the school culture. Where the non-conformists might escape the school's net, they cannot escape the exacting requirements of industry. Working values are brought back into the school to disqualify non-conformist behaviour. This often takes the form of a blackmail which says both that, 'If you are not developing the right attitudes now you will not succeed at work', and also more practically, 'If you do not co-operate now you will not get a good leaving report'. The totalising theme of preparation for work therefore often joins the embattled theme of 'co-operation', making the atmosphere positively reek with the gun smoke of moral indignation for the fifth year. Everything 'the lads' do seems to come back to their being selfish, rude and unco-operative, and, finally, damning to their future working lives.

Careers teacher to fifth year

I've just heard of a case, a lad at Easter, he got sacked after three weeks. He resented authority and wouldn't obey the rules. His attitude was wrong, the manager just sacked him, he said 'OUT', he wasn't going to put up with it, why should he? I've told you before, bad habits at school take a lot of throwing over. If you're resentful of authority here, and have a bad attitude towards discipline, it will carry on at work, it will show there and they won't have time for it. Now's the time to start making the effort, show you are up to it now . . . What you'll be doing is exchanging one lot of problems for another worse lot of problems (when you go to work), and they're all made by your own attitudes, your attitudes at school here now will make it that much harder for you when you get to work.*

Still, whether in new wave, 'progressive', modified or traditional mode, 'the lads' reject, ignore, invert, make fun of, or transform most of what they are given in careers lessons. The denoted level of straight exhortation to take getting a job seriously, to prepare carefully for interviews, and to push and achieve in the job, or even simple information about different jobs – apart perhaps from something they have already decided to do – is most heavily filtered.

[In a group discussion on careers sessions]

Spansky   After a bit you tek no notice of him, he sez the same thing over and over again, you know what I mean?

Joey   We're always too busy picking your nose, or flicking paper, we just don't listen to him.

*   From field notes, not transcription
. . . Material edited out
        P. Willis, *Learning to Labour*, 1977, pp. 91–2.

Questions
1. *What is the 'meritocratic model' to which Paul Willis refers (para. 1)?*
2. *Discuss the ways in which the values of the work situation are used by the teacher.*
3. *How would you account for 'the lads' rejection of careers lessons?*

AFTER SCHOOL: WHAT HAPPENS TO THE GIRLS?

There is relatively little evidence available that looks at the post-school careers of girls who leave school at sixteen. On the basis of a survey of 659 school leavers (337 boys and 322 girls) in Bradford, Helen Roberts considers what happens to girls and compares the experiences of girls and boys.

Reading 7

In the survey as a whole, the difference between boys and girls in terms of training were:

— 42 girls and 22 boys have a job which provides no training.
— 1 girl and 16 boys have block release for training.
— 21 girls and 29 boys have day release for training.
— 1 girl and 8 boys have a college training of between 6 and 12 months.
— 17 girls and 10 boys have some other kind of training (for example on the job).
— 49 boys and 8 girls have training which lasts between 3 and 5 years.

The notion of a 'career' is probably not an appropriate one for most of the girls going into employment at sixteen. The name of the game is getting a job, getting a wage, keeping off the dole.

Some of the interview material bears out Ashton and Maguire's (1980) observation that 'young people at school are all too well aware of the rules governing educational selection, but are largely ignorant of the rules governing selection in the labour market' (p. 157). While it was clear that for the high achievers, opportunity led to greater opportunity, for those girls who did less well, their worlds tended to shrink. What we know of sociological theories of socialisation and social control might lead us to think that we can explain patterns of female employment, but such theories would be inadequate. They might explain why things remain as they are, but not why they are as they are.

Sociological theories which are not informed by a feminist perspective might lead us, if we were conservative, to say, that is the way things are; this is one of the ways in which society maintains stability; women doing one sort of job and men doing another is functional. If we were more radical, theories of socialisation and social control might lead us to say that nothing can be changed until everything is changed.

Neither of these positions are very helpful to the young women who are now unemployed, in poorly paid jobs, or not getting any training. But sociological theorising on the nature of social change indicates that changes can and do take place. While the sociology of social change cannot be fully discussed here, it is clear that *structures of attitude and structures of opportunity reinforce each other*. Changes in either can lead to changes in the other. Any changes in the employment and opportunity patterns of girls – through, for instance, innovative YOP schemes of imaginative counselling from careers officers – will involve changes in the examples that are set before young women, and changes in the young women's conceptions of what is natural, normal and desirable. The consequences of small scale reforms are seldom therefore, limited to the immediate benefits which they secure. If one form of discrimination can reinforce another, so can opporutnity lead to more opportunity.

H. Roberts, 'After sixteen: what choice?' in R. G. Burgess (ed), *Exploring Society*, 1982, pp. 108–9.

Questions

1. *What does the reading reveal about patterns of employment and further training among sixteen-year old boys and girls in Bradford?*
2. *How would you explain the patterns of female employment using: (i) functionalist theory; (ii) sociological theories informed by a feminist perspective?*
3. *Do 'structures of attitude and structures of opportunity reinforce each other' (para. 4)? Illustrate your answer with reference to sixteen-year-old school-leavers.*

EDUCATION, EMPLOYMENT AND UNEMPLOYMENT

The destination for many school-leavers in the 1980s is as likely to be a training scheme of some description as it is a job. Using data from a survey in Scotland, Brian Main and David Raffe explore the relationship between educational qualifications and position in the labour market for a sample of boys and girls.

Reading 8

Table. Labour Market Status in October 1980 by sex, and SCE Qualifications

	Job	Unemployed	YOP	Total	Unweighted N
(a) Sex					
males (%)	62	18	20	100	(1580)
females (%)	59	19	21	99	(1488)
(b) SCE qualification					
Highers (%)	79	13	8	100	(593)
4+ O grades (A–C) (%)	78	12	10	100	(506)
1–3 O grades (A–C) (%)	62	14	23	99	(964)
D-E awards at O grade (%)	52	21	27	100	(334)
No SCE awards (%)	45	28	28	101	(671)

Note: SCE – Scottish Certificate of Education.

B. Main and D. Raffe, 'The "transition from school to work" in 1980/81: a dynamic account', in *British Educational Research Journal*, 1983, p. 61, table 1 (adapted).

Questions

1. *Summarise the pattern of the labour market status of males and females shown in this table.*
2. *Outline and discuss the relationship between educational qualifications and the labour market.*
3. *Are the labour market opportunities of school-leavers stratified according to educational qualifications? Give reasons for your answer.*

ESSAY QUESTIONS

1. It has been suggested that Functionalists and Marxists ask the same macro-sociological questions about education but come up with very different answers. With reference to one or more examples from your studies, illustrate this statement. Briefly comment on the adequacy of the answers they provide. (JMB, 1983)
2. 'The main function of schooling is to provide the economy with a ready, willing and able supply of workers.' Discuss. (AEB, 1980)
3. Is there a relationship between education and industrialisation?

4. Does the educational system facilitate the smooth transition of youth into the labour force?

FURTHER READING

1. G. H. Bantock, *Culture, Industrialisation and Education*, Faber, 1968.

   Argues that the early stages of industrialisation provided educational growth and the development of an educational system.

2. S. Bowles and H. Gintis, *Schooling in Capitalist America*, Routledge and Kegan Paul, 1976.

   Provides an account of the relationship between the American educational system and American economic life. For an analysis and a critique see Musgrove (1979) and Coles (1983) among many others. These sources are for advanced students.

3. B. R. Cosin (ed), *Education: Structure and Society*, Penguin, 1972.

   Part one of this book contains a range of short extracts on education and the economy using material from historical and contemporary sources. See especially the articles by Landes, Ashby and Galbraith.

4. R. Dale, G. Esland, R. Fergusson and M. MacDonald (eds), *Education and the State Volume I: Schooling and the National Interest*, Falmer Press, 1981.

   Section 2 contains papers on education, the economy and the labour process. See especially the extracts from Braverman, Sanderson and, for an overview of the education–industry debate, see the article by Reeder that was originally published in 1979.

5. G. Esland and H. Cathcart, 'Education and the corporate economy' in Open University, *The State and the Politics of Education* (Course E353, Block 1, Part 1, Unit 2)|Open University Press, 1981, pp. 57–100.

   Focuses on the relationship between education and the economy using pluralist and Marxist analyses. A good summary of positions with useful illustrative material.

6. D. Finn and S. Frith, 'Education and the labour market' in Open University, *The State and the Politics of Education* (Course E353, Block 1, Part 2, Unit 4) Open University Press, 1981, pp. 41–85.

   Examines the relationship between the education system and industry with special reference to Britain in the 1960s and 1970s – a useful complement to Esland and Cathcart.

7. A. H. Halsey, J. Floud and C. A. Anderson (eds), *Education, Economy and Society*, Free Press, 1961.

   A now classic collection of papers – see the introduction and part one for discussions of education and the economy from a functionalist perspective.

8. J. Karabel and A. H. Halsey (eds), *Power and Ideology in Education*, Oxford University Press, 1977.

Contains a long introduction on educational research. For a guide to functionalism and human capital theory see pp. 8–16 and for a critique of Bowles and Gintis see pp. 36–40.

9. A. Watts, *Education, Unemployment and the Future of Work*, Open University Press, 1983.

   Chapters 1 and 2 provide a good account of the relationship between education and employment and education and unemployment. It is clearly written.

10. P. Willis, *Learning to Labour*, Saxon House, 1977.

    An ethnographic account of the relationship between school and work among a group of boys that has been written from a Marxist perspective.

3
Education and the structure of opportunity

Among the most well-trodden paths in the sociology of education is that area of research and writing that concerns itself with equality of educational opportunity. With the expansion of educational provision in the 1950s and 1960s, sociologists explored the effects of these educational developments on equality of opportunity. Meanwhile, more recent reviews from a Marxist perspective have explored some of the links between education and social inequality. No matter what perspective is taken, there are several conceptual issues that need to be identified and discussed. First, the meaning of equality and inequality. Secondly, the meaning of equality of educational opportunity. Thirdly, the way in which researchers have defined social class in examining patterns of educational inequality and trends in social mobility. Such issues are sufficient to mark this out as an area of considerable controversy.

Among the questions that sociologists have addressed are: do schools help to create a society open to talent? Have schools provided a channel of social mobility? Have schools helped to promote equality or to heighten inequality? No matter what explanations are provided by empirical evidence, they give rise to further questions concerning the extent to which equality of educational opportunity has been achieved, the extent to which the gap has been narrowed between the working class and the middle class, between pupils that are black and those that are white, and between boys and girls. In turn, sociologists have also gone on to speculate about the implications of recent trends in equality of educational opportunity. It is the purpose of this chapter to consider some of the main areas of research and writing on this subject in order to highlight some of the debates and controversies not only concerning the trends, patterns and processes of education, but also those surrounding the concepts and studies themselves.

We begin by looking at some of the arguments concerning education that were advanced by R. H. Tawney in his collection of essays on *Equality* (1964) that were originally published in the early 1930s. Tawney's position was very clear concerning the way he perceived the educational system in England at the time, when he stated that 'the hereditary curse upon English education is its organization upon lines of social class'. Tawney was writing in a period before universal compulsory secondary education was made available to all under the provisions of the 1944 Education Act. The question that has subsequently been posed by generations of sociologists and other commentators on the educational scene is the extent to which equal opportunity has been achieved in England in the post-1944 era. Among the major works that are involved with this issue is the study by Halsey, Heath and Ridge entitled *Origins and Destinations* (1980). Drawing on evidence from their study of 10,000 adult males in England and Wales they have been able to make comparisons not only between classes but also between generations concerning the notion 'equality of educational opportunity'. While many have applauded the range of evidence that Halsey and his colleagues have brought together and the ways in which they have advanced the debate, others have been more critical and pointed to some of the limitations associated with this study and the caution that needs to be exercised in interpreting the results. Among reviews of this study, Tessa Blackstone's remarks on the ways in which the questions that were posed influenced the analysis are particularly useful. In turn, she points to some of the gaps that are present in this study, especially concerning the absence of girls and women.

Many studies not only omit girls and women but also ethnic minority groups. However, a major piece of research that looks at equality of educational opportunity for ethnic minorities as well as white pupils is the Coleman Report (1966) in the USA. In Reading 4 there is a brief summary of Coleman's findings which have not only been the subject of controversy among academics but also among policy-makers in the USA. A further study from the USA that has also been at the centre of debate is the work of Christopher Jencks (1972), which is also summarised here. Like Coleman's work, Jencks's evidence has been subject to further research about the significance of schooling in achieving equality of educational opportunity.

A further account from the USA that has had a major influence on sociological studies of education is Turner's analysis of the modes of mobility that characterise educational systems. While his analysis has been the subject of criticism and debate by Hopper (1971), it has been used by many sociologists. But we might ask how far does Turner's analysis of the English school system apply to trends and developments in contemporary Britain? Trends in social mobility have for some years figured in the sociological debate about education and opportunity. Evidence on the relationship between education and the class structure is available from a series of studies that were edited by Glass in the 1950s, although they have been critically reviewed by Musgrove (1979). More recent evidence from the Oxford Mobility Study has produced a set of data that Halsey uses to focus on recent trends in the relationship between education and mobility among members of the male population. This evidence shows that those individuals in the higher occupational categories have more education and more qualifications than those in lower occupational groups. In particular, Halsey examines the movement between the working class and the middle class through the educational system.

While trends in patterns of mobility are of interest, they are not the complete story. What, for example, has been the experience of the socially mobile? Here, we can turn to autobiographical accounts and in particular to Irene Payne's analysis of her experiences in a grammar school, an account that highlights the importance of class and gender. Finally, Westergaard and Resler's discussion raises a series of issues that arise from patterns of inequality in educational opportunity and social mobility that are still open to speculation and demand further research.

EQUALITY IN EDUCATION?

The material contained in this reading was originally delivered in a lecture given in 1929 in which R. H. Tawney addressed fundamental issues about the condition of British society. Among the issues covered were the problems surrounding equal opportunity in education – a topic that has subsequently become a central concern for sociologists of education.

Reading 1

The hereditary curse upon English education is its organization upon lines of social class. 'An elementary school education,' remarked recently an experienced educational administrator, 'has always meant, and still means, a cheap education. An elementary school text-book means a cheap book, which is carefully adapted in language and content to a wholly derogatory estimate of the needs and powers of the children of a certain section of society, who are supposed not to require or to be capable of the same kind of education as the children of parents who have more money.' The effect of the conditions as to staffing and accommodation still permitted to continue in many primary schools is not merely to cripple the performance of the vital and delicate task on which these schools are engaged. It is to poison their soul. It is to cause, not only their external organization, but their spirit and temper to be smitten by a blight of social inferiority.

Children are apt to think of themselves as their elders show that they think of them. The public school boy is encouraged to regard himself as one of a ruling class, which in politics, administration and business will govern and direct – to acquire, in short, the aristocratic virtues of initiative and self-reliance, as well as frequently the aristocratic vices of arrogance, intellectual laziness and self-satisfaction. The age of spiritual bobbing and curtseying in public education is, happily, over. The elementary schools, with all their defects, have done more than any other institution to straighten the backs of the mass of the population. But, while the theory that the standards permissible in element-ary schools ought to be inferior, because they are designed for a class which is inferior, is, if not dead, at any rate dying, the fact of their inferiority is only too alive. If the elementary school boy is no longer taught by his masters that the world has been divided by Providence into the rich, who are the ends of civilization, and the poor, who are its instruments, he is frequently taught a not very different lesson by the character of the surroundings which his countrymen provide for him.

He is taught it by mean, and in some cases even unhealthy, buildings; by the deficiency of playing-fields, school libraries, laboratories, and facilities for practical work; by the shortage of books themselves and the parsimony which holds that less than 2s. a year for each pupil is enough to spend on them. He is taught it by the persistent under-staffing which still permits the existence of 46,000 classes with over forty pupils on the register, and actually over 3,000 classes with more than fifty. He is taught it by his premature plunge into wage-earning employment and the conditions that he meets there. He is taught it by recurrent gusts of educational economy, with their ostentatious insistence that it is his happiness and his welfare which, when the ship is labouring, are the superfluity to be jettisoned. He is taught it by the naïve assurance with which his masters, unenlightened by a century of experience, persist in asserting that they cannot dispense with his immature labour, as though, while their own children continue their education to sixteen or twenty, he and his kind were predestined by Providence to be the cannon-fodder of industry. He is taught it, not least, by the very tenor of the proposals which are applauded as impressive reforms by his well-wishers themselves.

For consider the assumptions implied in the view hitherto held of the scope and purpose of secondary education. When the boys and girls of well-to-do parents attain the great age of thirteen to fourteen, no one asks whether – absurd phrase – they are 'capable of profiting' by further education. They continue their education as a matter of course, not because they are exceptional, but because they are normal, and the question of the 'profit' which they succeed in deriving from it is left, quite rightly, to be answered later. Working-class children have the same needs to be met, and the same powers to be developed. But their opportunities of developing them are rationed, like bread in a famine, under stringent precautions, as though, were secondary education made too accessible, the world would end – as it is possible, indeed, that one sort of world might.

Public opinion is so saturated with the influence of a long tradition of educational inequality, so wedded to the idea that what is obtained by one class without question must be conceded to another only on proof of special capacity, that eminent personages can still sometimes be heard to congratulate the nation on the existence of what they describe as an educational ladder, which has as its effect that less than one child in seven of those leaving the elementary schools wins access after being strained at eleven through the sieve of a competitive examination, to the secondary education that the children of the rich receive, in most cases, as a matter of course.

R. H. Tawney, *Equality*, 1964 (originally published in 1931), pp. 142–4.

Questions
1. *What relationship did Tawney perceive between social class and education?*
2. *Critically evaluate the evidence that Tawney provides on inequality in education in the 1930s.*
3. *To what extent do you agree with Tawney's view that in the 1930s 'the hereditary curse upon English education is its organization upon lines of social class' (para. 1)? Give reasons for your answer.*
4. *Can Tawney's analysis be applied to English education in the 1980s? Give reasons for your answer.*

EQUALITY OF OPPORTUNITY IN ENGLISH EDUCATION

Among the most recent assessments of the English educational system is the study *Origins and Destinations*, which examines equality of opportunity, meritocracy and the operation of the tripartite system of secondary education. The findings are derived from a sample of 10,000 adult men in England and Wales.

Reading 2

Equality of opportunity is a phrase with many different meanings. A minimal definition of it can be described as formal equality of opportunity with the implication that no legal barrier exists to prevent a child from entering any form of education in the way that Jews were once kept out of Oxford and Cambridge, or black Africans are excluded from white South African universities. In this minimal sense formal equality of opportunity existed in the British schools throughout our period. The real debate, at least in the years before 1944, turned on strengthening the definition to take account of inequalities of circumstances, and especially financial ones. It was these, whether in the form of school fees or earnings forgone where boys stayed on beyond the statutory leaving age, that were in dispute: and the 1944 Act brought the final elimination of fee paying in state selective secondary schools. If, therefore, we define equality of opportunity in a second way to include the elimination of financial barriers then the reduction of these through the expansion of free places before 1944 and their total abolition after 1944 was clear progress towards equality of opportunity. At the same time, however, the existence of the private sector at both primary and secondary level, and the absence of maintenance grants for secondary-school children beyond the statutory school-leaving age, prevented full realization of this stronger definition of the ideal aimed at through liberal reform.

It is also important and relevant to this second definition of equality of opportunity to notice the financial implications of a developing non-financial selective system. As we have seen, the 1944 Act continued the growth of selective secondary schooling and, particularly in the 1960s, there was expansion of higher education on a selective basis. The costs of the different forms of education have been such that success in the selective process did not diminish but, if anything, widened the distance between those who got most and those who got least out of the public purse towards the cost of their schooling.

Given, then, that the selective stakes became, if anything, higher it is all the more crucial to note the actual distribution

between social classes of educational costs, educational experience and examination results. In consequence, the third
definition of equality of opportunity on which we have concentrated is one which compares the relative chances of access to
schools and qualifications which were, *substantively* as distinct
from *formally*, open to the children of different social classes. In
effect, taking the word 'equality' to have its normal meaning in
common speech, the definition now shifts from equality of
opportunity to equality of outcome.

This third meaning of equality of opportunity in the sense of
equality of access to superior forms of education yields a much
less comforting picture. At the secondary-school stage access has
been more unequal at the higher levels of the academic hierarchy
as we have defined it. Class differentials are most extreme in the
case of the independent HMC schools; a boy from the service
class had nearly forty times the chance of his working-class peer
of entering one of these schools. In the case of the Direct Grant
schools his chance was twelve times as good, and in that of the
grammar schools it was three times as good. Only in the technical
schools has there been equality of class chances, and even this
apparently more equitable distribution of opportunity has had
much more to do with their lower standing in the academic
pecking order than with the fairness of their methods of
selection; relatively few boys from the service class went to the
technical schools simply because so many had already gone to
notionally superior secondary schools.

In general, then, class chances of access vary according to
position in the academic hierarchy. The only clear exception is
that of the minor independent schools. We have ranked these
below the grammar schools (a position confirmed by their O-
Level and A-Level records), but the service-class boy had nearly
eighteen times the chance of the working-class boy of securing a
place at one. Another possible exception is that of the major
independent schools. We placed these at the head of the
academic hierarchy. Though on most criteria of academic
achievement they are virtually indistinguishable from the Direct
Grant schools, they are socially far more exclusive. The private
schools represent a bastion of class privilege compared with the
relatively egalitarian state sector. The hybrid Direct Grant
schools, before they were abolished, uncomfortably straddled the
divide.

Class differentials in access are necessarily reflected in school differences of class composition. Only the technical schools contained anything resembling a representative cross-section of the population, while the HMC schools remained socially the most exclusive. About 90 per cent of those at the private schools came from the service and intermediate classes. In contrast, over one-third of boys in the state grammar schools came from the working class. Admittedly, the grammar schools may have served more to assimilate these working-class boys into middle-class life and culture than to break down class boundaries, but the social experience they offered must undoubtedly have been significantly different from that of the private sector. Tawney's judgement accordingly retains its force:

> A special system of schools, reserved for children whose parents have larger bank accounts than their neighbours, exists in no other country on the same scale as in England. It is at once an educational monstrosity and a grave national misfortune. It is educationally vicious, since to mix with companions from homes of different types is an important part of the education of the young. It is socially disastrous for it does more than any other single cause, except capitalism itself, to perpetuate the division of the nation into classes of which one is almost unintelligible to the other.
>
> A. H. Halsey, A. F. Heath and J. M. Ridge, *Origins and Destinations: Family, Class and Education in Modern Britain*, 1980, pp. 201–3.

Questions

1. *Compare and contrast the meanings of the term 'equality of opportunity' in this reading. How useful do you find this term in discussing education?*
2. *Why do you think the writers consider that their third meaning of 'equality of opportunity' yields a less comforting picture than the previous two? Can you provide further evidence to support or refute their judgement?*
3. *Do you feel that the evidence produced by the writers supports Tawney's views?*

ORIGINS AND DESTINATIONS: A REVIEW

Most major studies in sociology are subject to review, criticism, discussion and debate. In this respect *Origins and Destinations* by Halsey and his colleagues was no exception. Among the reviews that were provided, Tessa Blackstone's discussion placed the work in context, evaluated the findings and discussed gaps in the questions posed.

Reading 3

There is a considerable literature on education and equality, most of it written in the past two decades. Many contemporary social scientists have been fascinated by this relationship. Sociologists in particular have written extensively about it, often examining it as a facet of the study of social stratification. *Origins and Destinations* is the latest contribution to these writings. And it should be said at the outset that it is a distinguished and distinctive contribution.

As the authors themselves point out, it is a study in the tradition of political arithmetic which goes back to Mayhew, Booth and the Webbs, and more recently to David Glass's work on social mobility at the London School of Economics in the late 1940s and early 1950s. It is, however, distinctive in its attempt to use quantitative data from a large sample to throw light on the validity of certain theories, in particular those of the French sociologist Pierre Bourdieu. It also makes use of a number of sophisticated modern statistical techniques, not available when the last large-scale survey of this type in Britain was undertaken by Glass.

The sample is of 10,000 men aged between 20 and 64 and living in England and Wales in 1972. The nature of the sample provides the first important criticism of not just this book but its companion volume by John Goldthorpe on *Social Mobility and Class Structure* and the subsequent studies that are in the pipeline based on this survey. It is confined to men. The rationale for this was that Glass's study was based on a sample of men as was Blau and Duncan's major study of mobility in the USA in the 1960s. In order to make comparisons with Britain over two different periods and between Britain and America – major goals of the wider study – data about women would be unnecessary, indeed useless. This is not altogether convincing.

The inclusion of women in the sample would not have prevented such comparisons, since data on them could easily have been eliminated from that part of the analysis. There are two senses in which their exclusion is a matter of real regret. First, it is not possible to see from this sample how they have progressed during the past 40 years in terms of educational opportunities and how any such progress compares to that of men. Second, it means that the next major mobility survey in 10 or 15 years time, which will surely include women, will not be able to make any comparisons with the findings of this study as far as half the population is concerned. Since one of the most important social changes of the last decade has concerned the educational and occupational advance of women which seems highly likely to be maintained, if not increased, over the next decade, this is a great pity.

The data itself is limited to a fairly small number of questions about the education of the respondent, such as the type of school attended at both the primary and secondary stage, school-leaving age and qualifications and post-school education. No data of a qualitative kind such as attitudinal questions was collected. The fact that the survey was not designed as a study primarily about education but about social mobility explains this. It does however mean that at times the authors have had to stretch their data by, for example, the use of proxies and other ingenious methods to answer the questions they pose.

It is useful to list these questions in the authors' own words:

1. What have been the class differences in access to education?

2. How far has the British educational system achieved its goal on meritocracy?

3. What are the handicaps which prevent individuals attaining educational success?

4. What are the likely consequences of comprehensive reform for the achievement of goals such as equality of opportunity and equality of results?

5. Is the structure of the educational system important?

The key question to which the authors devote the most attention is the first. They also ask how far these differences have changed over time and whether changes in policy, particularly those associated with the 1944 Act and general educational expansion, have led to greater equality of class chances. Some of their most interesting and controversial analysis concerns the second question, where they attempt to quantify the degree to which mid twentieth-century Britain has selected its young people for elite forms of education according to merit. The third and fourth questions pose the biggest problems since the limitations of their data handicap the authors in answering them.

T. Blackstone, 'Falling short of meritocracy', *The Times Higher Education Supplement*, 18 January 1980, p. 14.

Questions

1. *What problems does Blackstone associate with the fact that women were excluded from the sample studied? Do you agree with her assessment? Give reasons for your answer.*

2. *How has the focus on social mobility influenced the educational questions posed in the study?*

3. *Suggest reasons why an analysis of the extent to which the English educational system has achieved the goal of meritocracy might be contentious.*

EQUALITY OF EDUCATIONAL OPPORTUNITY IN THE USA

In common with sociologists in Britain, American sociologists of education have focused on equality of educational opportunity. Two major studies that have contributed to our understanding of inequality and stimulated much research and debate on both sides of the Atlantic are by Coleman and others on *Equality of Educational Opportunity* (1966) and by Jencks and his associates on *Inequality* (1972). They both challenge strongly-held assumptions.

Reading 4

The purpose of the [Coleman report] was to evaluate opportunities and performance of minority students compared with white students. Coleman's survey extended to about 5 percent of the schools in the U.S. and covered 645,000 students at five grade levels. The children were given tests of several types; information about the children's backgrounds and attitudes was collected; and school administrators filled out questionnaires about their schools. Coleman's findings revealed that: 1) Minority students (except for Oriental-Americans) scored lower on tests at each level of schooling than did white students, and that this disparity increased from the first to twelfth grades. Coleman attributed the disadvantage of minority students to a combination of out-of-school factors, many of which center in the family: poverty, parents' education, and other environmental factors. 2) The majority of children at the time of the report attended segregated schools. Teachers also tended to teach children of their own race. 3) The socioeconomic makeup of the school, the home background, and the background of other students in the school were factors which made the biggest difference in students' school achievement levels. This was a surprising finding and led to the recommendation that schools should be integrated, in order to have a racial-class mix of students. 4) Curriculum and facilities made little difference in student achievement levels – another surprising finding. In fact, school facilities turned out to differ very little across predominantly black or white schools. 5) White children had somewhat greater access to physics, chemistry, language labs, text books, college curricula, and better qualified and higher paid teachers, but the differences were not very great.

These findings have been tested and retested by researchers, and while there are variations in the results, Coleman's general conclusions have been upheld. It was these findings which led to Coleman's recommendation that one way to improve the academic achievement of poor and minority children would be to integrate the schools, putting minority children with white children to produce a climate for achievement and to provide educational role models. The study provided the impetus for increased efforts to desegregate, especially through the use of busing.

Jencks' study of inequality. Another famous and often quoted study questions the use of schools to attain equal opportunity in society. Christopher Jencks argues that no evidence suggests that school reform can bring about significant social changes outside schools:

> the evidence suggests that equalizing educational opportunity would do very little to make adults more equal. If all elementary schools were equally effective, cognitive inequality among sixth-graders would decline less than three percent . . . cognitive inequality among twelfth-graders would hardly decline at all, and disparities in their eventual attainment would decline less than one percent. Eliminating all economic and academic obstacles to college attendance might somewhat reduce disparities in educational attainment, but the change would not be large. (Aronson, 1978, p. 409)

Jencks points out that experience over the past twenty-five years suggests that even when the educational attainment gap between minorities and whites is narrowed, economic inequalty among adults continues to exist.

Jencks concludes that schools can do little to change people's status in society after graduation. Even school reform and compensatory education programs are not seen as effective in substantially changing the differences between adults. These conclusions both startled and angered educators and others; it is not pleasant to hear that *schools make little difference*. In this study, Jencks does not deny that schools are important for everyone – he did say that they cannot solve society's problems. He also concludes, as did Coleman, that the school achievement of children is dependent on one major factor – their families. Family background and attitudes toward education are primary determinants of school experience. Jencks argues that since schools cannot achieve an egalitarian society and economic equality, we must redistribute income by changing the economic institution into a more socialistic system.

While the tests and retests of Coleman's and Jencks' conclusions come up with varied results, most uphold the importance of students' families and backgrounds of peers.

> J. H. Ballantine, *The Sociology of Education: A Systematic Analysis*, 1983, pp. 86–8.

Questions
1. *In what ways can Coleman's evidence contribute to our understanding of the relationship between education and social inequality?*
2. *On what basis does Jencks conclude that 'schools make little difference' (para. 4)?*
3. *Compare and contrast the findings of Coleman and Jencks in terms of equality of educational opportunity.*

MODES OF SOCIAL MOBILITY

Among the most well-known papers in the sociology of education is Ralph Turner's comparative analysis of educational systems in England and the United States. His focus of interest is the mode of upward mobility in societies. His paper contrasts the characteristics of sponsored mobility in England and contest mobility in the United States.

Reading 5

Two ideal-typical organizing norms concerning the manner in which mobility should properly take place have been outlined. On the one hand, mobility may be viewed as most appropriately a *contest* in which many contestants strive, by whatever combinations of strategy, enterprise, perseverance, and ability they can marshal, restricted only by a minimum set of rules defining fair play and minimizing special advantage to those who get ahead early in the game, to take possession of a limited number of prizes. On the other hand, it may be thought best that the upwardly mobile person be *sponsored*, like one who joins a private club upon invitation of the membership, selected because the club members feel that he has qualities desirable in a club member, and then subjected to careful training and initiation into the guiding ethic and lore of the club before being accorded full membership.

Upward mobility actually takes place to a considerable degree by both the contest pattern and the sponsorship pattern in every society. But it has been suggested that in England the sponsorship norm is ascendant and has been so for a century or more, and that in the United States the contest norm has been ascendant for a comparable period. A norm is ascendant in the sense that there is a constant 'strain' to bring the relevant features of the class system, the pattern of social control, and the educational system into consistency with the norm, and that patterns consistent with the ascendant norm seem more 'natural' and 'right' to the articulate segments of the population.

The statement has been broadly impressionistic and speculative, reflecting more the over-all impression of an observer of both countries than a systematic exploration of data. Relevant data of a variety of sorts have been cited, but their use has been more illustrative than demonstrative. Several lines of research are suggested by the statement. One of these is an exploration of different channels of mobility in both countries to discover the extent to which mobility corresponds to each of the types. Recruitment to the Catholic priesthood, for example, probably follows a strictly sponsorship norm regardless of the dominant contest norm in the United States.

The effect of changes in the major avenues of upward mobility upon the dominant norms requires investigation. The increasing importance of promotion through corporation hierarchies and the declining importance of the entrepreneurial path to upward mobility undoubtedly compromise the ideal pattern of contest mobility. The increasing insistence upon higher education as a prerequisite to a variety of employments is a similar modification. On the other hand, there is little evidence of a tendency to follow the logic of sponsorship beyond the bureaucratic selection process. The prospect of a surplus of college-educated persons in relation to jobs requiring college education tends to restore the contest situation at a higher level, and the further fact that completion of higher education may be more determined by motivational factors than by capacity suggests that the contest pattern continues within the school.

In England, on the other hand, two developments may dull the distinctive edge of the sponsorship system. One is response to popular demand to allow more children to secure the grammar-school type of training, particularly through including such a program in the secondary modern schools. The other is introduction of the comprehensive secondary school, relatively uncommon at present but a major plank in the Labour party's education platform. It remains to be determined whether the comprehensive school in England will take a distinctive form and serve a distinctive function that preserves the pattern of sponsorship or whether it will approximate the present American system.

Finally, the assertion that these types are embedded in genuine folk norms requires specific investigation. A combination of direct study of popular attitudes and content analysis of popular responses to crucial issues is necessary. Perhaps the most significant search would be for evidence showing what courses of action seem to require no special justification or explanation because they are altogether 'natural' and 'right,' and which courses of action, whether approved or not, seem to require special justification and explanation. Such evidence, appropriately used, would permit study of the extent to which the patterns described are genuine folk norms rather than the mere by-product of particular structural factors in society. It would also permit determination of the extent to which acceptance of the ascendant folk norm is diffused among the varied segments of the population.

R. H. Turner, 'Sponsored and contest mobility and the school system', in A. H. Halsey, J. Floud and C. A. Anderson (eds), *Education, Economy and Society*, 1961, pp. 135–7.

Questions
1. *Compare and contrast 'sponsored' and 'contest' mobility.*
2. *Do you think the expansion of comprehensive education in England has influenced the pattern of social mobility? Give reasons for your answer.*

3. *Turner suggests various issues that demand investigation. Take one of the issues that Turner has identified and discuss the way in which you would design an inquiry into the problem.*

EDUCATION AND SOCIAL MOBILITY IN ENGLAND

The way in which patterns of social mobility relate to education in England was originally discussed by Glass and his colleagues in the book *Social Mobility* (1954), a study that has subsequently been superseded by the Oxford Mobility Study (Goldthorpe, 1980). In this reading Halsey utilises the Oxford study to comment on relationships between education and mobility in England.

Reading 6

The educational profiles of the nine mobility categories, apart from yielding recognizable stereotypes of Britons, show a regular patterning of the relations between education and mobility. It can be seen from the italicized rows of [the] Table that the educational norms for each of the three social classes, as represented by those who have had stable membership, are positively related to social class both of origin and destination. Thus the stable middle-class men are composed of 88 per cent with selective secondary schooling and 30 per cent with a university education, compared with 44 and 1 per cent for the stable lower middle class, and 15 and 0·1 per cent for the stable working class. In other words, those who find jobs in the higher occupational categories have more education and more qualifications. This will surprise no one.

Looking at the other six categories of those who have moved from their birth position it is equally clear that mobility involves realignment of social-class membership according to educational qualifications. Thus those who have moved upwards have, in the process, exceeded the educational norms of their origin group, and those who have moved downwards have had less educational advantage and attained fewer educational qualifications. This pattern is absolutely regular. But there are some details worth remarking. If we look at the destination classes it appears that those who move up from below do not, on average, have as much educational qualification as those who have been stable in the

Table. Education and Mobility (%)

Class	Private primary schooling	Selective secondary schooling	School examinations	Some further-education qualifications	University degree
1. *Stable middle class*	*32.0*	*88.4*	*82.0*	*33.1*	*29.8*
2. Middle	24.9	65.1	53.6	17.2	5.7
3. Middle to working	3.8	33.5	15.1	7.0	0.5
4. Lower middle to working	11.7	67.9	62.1	34.1	13.5
5. *Stable lower middle*	*7.5*	*44.3*	*27.1*	*5.6*	*1.0*
6. Lower middle to working	3.0	21.9	8.1	1.8	0.1
7. Working to middle	1.6	63.1	58.5	32.3	12.8
8. Working to lower middle	2.0	32.2	20.2	3.9	1.1
9. *Stable working*	*0.6*	*14.7*	*4.6*	*0.4*	*0.1*
ALL	5.8	34.8	23.9	10.3	4.3

destination class in question. Similarly, those who move down still have a rather higher educational profile than the stable members of the class they join and, which follows from our remarks on the upwardly mobile, a still higher one than those who have joined the same destination class from below.

Putting these two tendencies together, i.e. the association of education with social origin and also its association with mobility, what we then find is that exchange between the social classes is also a partial exchange of the educationally qualified. For example, those who have moved from the middle class to the working class include only 1 per cent of graduates, while those who have moved from the working class to the middle class include 13 per cent of graduates. There is thus, in the process of mobility, exchange not only of individuals but of social invest-ment of education and qualifications which maintains a differen-tial distribution of social qualities between the social classes. I would lay particular emphasis on this aspect of the reproduction of the stratification system. Intergenerational mobility serves to reconstitute the general pattern of distribution of attributes of the different social classes.

> A. H. Halsey, 'Social mobility and education', in D. Rubinstein (ed), *Education and Equality*, 1979, pp. 61–2.

Questions

1. *What does Halsey conclude about (i) those who have moved upwards; (ii) those who have moved downwards?*
2. *Do you find Halsey's explanations about education and social mobility plausible? Give reasons for your answer.*
3. *Outline and discuss the relationship between educational qualifications and the process of social mobility.*

A WORKING-CLASS GIRL IN A GRAMMAR SCHOOL

There are relatively few accounts of how the socially mobile have handled and been handled by schools and by the educational system. Irene Payne provides an autobiographical account of her grammar school education in which she highlights the imposition of middle-class values and the social divisions based on social class and gender in a grammar school.

Reading 7

Implicitly and explicitly we were inculcated with our role in the 'art of conversation' which encouraged us not only to be correct (as no doubt working-class boys would be encouraged in the grammar school) but also polite and deferential (an attribute not necessarily encouraged among boys). My grammar school education reveals a *class* and a *gender ideology* at work on my language.

I managed to conform and meet the linguistic requirements of the school, but they could only be used within the school. I had to abandon them when I left the school gates and had to change my language for home. Such 'bilingualism' is not without its disadvantages and can work to make one feel inadequate and unconfident in all language use. Mistakes at school could be an offence, but so too could mistakes at home. I was in constant terror of being exposed as a 'freak'. My way of dealing with this threat was to over-react. In my home environment I made a concerted effort to appear as 'one of the girls' and to do this I felt obliged to be louder than anyone else, to swear more, just to prove I wasn't different and hadn't been corrupted by the grammar school.

It was like leading a double life, for neither side would have recognised me in the other context. I was straddling two very different worlds and felt considerably threatened by the fact that I didn't belong to either. I had a constant sense of being different, which I interpreted as inferiority. I was always aware of the possibility of making a mistake and being exposed as fraudulent. I could not relax in either setting. I had a sense of inferiority within school because I didn't come from such a "good' background as most of the other pupils. I was always uneasy when people began to parade their status symbols and discuss their father's occupations and where they lived. At school I felt ashamed of my background and attempted to conceal it. My Dad was a manual worker and we were pretty poor and I didn't want my classmates to know this. Nor did I want them to know that I lived in a 'rough' area, in a house that didn't have a bathroom.

At the same time I didn't want my friends in my neighbourhood to know that I was considered clever at school. (It is not of course unusual for some working-class kids who have received scholarships to be diagnosed in this way. One 'clever' working-class student vindicates the whole system and attests to the myth of equality of opportunity. However, it places enormous demands on such students.) In order not to be dismissed by my out-of-school friends I pretended that school was unimportant; I gave the impression that I didn't care about it. This of course demanded many subterfuges on my part. Life was a juggling process. Homework, for example, was difficult for me as I did not want my friends to know that I did it (I could not have preserved the belief that I didn't care about school if I indicated that I conscientiously did my homework). Because I didn't want my friends thinking I was a 'swot' (and withdrawing their friendship as a result) I tried to get all my homework finished before they came to call for me.

With my girlfriends the problems associated with school success were class ones and so that I could retain their friendship I disguised my attitude to school. But there are gender as well as class dimensions to this problem for it wasn't just with my girlfriends that I felt obliged to hide my school achievements. The problem of being seen as clever was particularly acute when it came to having boyfriends. I thought that being regarded as intelligent would make me less attractive to boys. I was always careful, therefore, to make light of my grammar school education and to refrain from mentioning how many O levels I was doing. Again there was the fear of making a mistake for, to me, it seemed that it would be a mistake to be seen as being more clever than a boy.

The pressures on me were conflicting and varied. For quite a while I tried to negotiate two worlds, but the time came when such negotiation was no longer possible. The two worlds proved to be incompatible. The two sets of values ordained different futures and the point came where I had to decide which future would be mine. Eventually the pull of the school was stronger for it held out the promise of social mobility through higher education. Once I decided to stay on at school after the statutory leaving age my fate was sealed. I could no longer pretend that school was unimportant or irrelevant. It was clear to my friends at home that I had marked myself as 'different' and from this point our paths were to diverge. They entered the world of paid work and they left me behind; I could not disguise myself as one of them any more.

I think that my experience shows that working-class values are not readily accommodated within the middle-class culture of schools. It is not possible to incorporate both sets of values, for the conflict between them is too great. In trying to conform to the requirements of the school I ultimately had to live the ideology encompassed within the school and this meant rejecting many of the values of my home. This is not the experience of working-class kids in general because they are not singled out for school success. Realistically, working-class kids have few expectations of education as a means of transforming their lives. They continue to live out the values which will ensure their existence as workers for capitalism.

My experience as a working-class girl contained more contradictions than that of my middle-class peers whose culture more closely approximated that of the school. However, there were contradictions shared and the organisation of the curriculum provides an example of sexist ideology at work. In my school there was an academic ethos and this meant that practical subjects were accorded low status. While this is an aspect of bourgeois ideology which constructs the mental/manual division of labour, it is also an example of patriarchal ideology with its direct relationship to the sexual division of labour in our society.

I. Payne, 'A working class girl in a grammar school', in D. Spender and E. Sarah (eds), *Learning to Lose: Sexism and Education*, 1980, pp. 16–18.

Questions

1. *Examine the conflicts that Irene Payne found between: (i) home and school; (ii) her peers and her school. Does her account relate to your experience of schooling?*
2. *What do you understand by the following terms: (i) class ideology; (ii) gender ideology (para. 1)? Discuss the ways in which they can be used to examine your education.*
3. *Are working-class values accommodated in schools? Give reasons for your answer.*

MOBILITY AND EDUCATIONAL OPPORTUNITY: SOME IMPLICATIONS

Although there has been considerable research and writing on trends in social mobility and educational opportunity, there is relatively little work on the consequences of these social processes for the way in which people perceive their class situation, their life-chances and the experience of social mobility. Westergaard and Resler have therefore provided some speculative comments.

Reading 8

With the deliberate direction of schools and colleges to the business of selection, institutional provision has been made for social circulation: the educational system provides a commonly recognized machinery for the purpose. This in turn may well have consequences for the ways in which people see their class situation, assess their chances in life, react to the experience of social mobility or immobility. Such consequences, however, are as yet largely a matter for speculation.

One may have been to transfer some part of the burden of worries associated with mobility – and with hopes or fears of mobility in the future – from the shoulders of the mobile themselves to those of their parents. The child who is upwardly mobile through educational success moves upwards in the company of others, in a series of steps that are well marked and institutionally established. The risk of failure in the competition is usually with him throughout his schooling. He is not guaranteed a place in the élite from an early age, as one fashionable characterization of educational mobility in this country as 'sponsored' implies. Even so, the path to success is more clearly mapped and visible, even predictable on well-known conditions, than was that of the man who made his own way in business from modest beginnings or, say, of a clerk in whose promotion luck and patronage played a large part. Those who climb through the educational system may therefore need to use their elbows, and to set a symbolic distance between themselves and their origins, less than many who climbed by other means in the past. To that extent, the familiar syndrome of the *nouveaux riches* may be less typical than it was. There is, moreover, evidence to suggest that parents take on a good deal of the load which might otherwise be carried by their sons and daughters *en route* to higher levels of the class hierarchy. Those working-class children who get into, and stay the course of, academic education come disproportionately from families who differ from the ordinary run of manual workers in some of their characteristics. They come from smaller families than the manual average, on the whole; from families in which husband, wife or both not only have fairly high aspirations on behalf of their children, but also have ties in their own past history with the 'middle classes' – by way of origin and education – more often than other manual couples. For all that, however, they may find it difficult to keep up with their children; to understand the world into which these are moving, as they climb the ladder of achievement at school and college. These parents, more than their successful children, may truly be 'marginal': neither fully working class nor 'middle class' except in vague aspiration.

It is possible that, as more mobility is channelled through the educational system, personal failure in life by conventional criteria may be more likely to be accepted by the individuals concerned, as a matter for resignation rather than resentment or protest. Justice might be believed to be done – though it is often not done – because educational testing is ostensibly fair. Moreover, the chances of social ascent may be thought of as greater than they are – and as much greater than in the past, though they are not – because the educational system provides a visible and institutionally established machinery of social circulation. All this is conceivable. But it is again speculation. And the arguments, without hard facts, can cut both ways.

Just because schools and colleges now are geared to social

selection; just because the declared aim of the political establishment is to make that process of selection both fair and efficient – aspirations are likely to be raised: and to levels, perhaps, where their clash with the reality of limited opportunities may become acute. The signs are that working-class parents have a high, and increasing, interest in their children's education – because they are aware of, and may indeed overestimate, the dependence of individual prospects in life on schooling. Typically, however, they lack the means – cultural as well as material, indirect as well as direct – to translate that interest into effective influence on their children's behalf. The result may well be growing consciousness of the ways in which the dice are loaded against their sons and daughters; and such consciousness may be made more potent by the knowledge that they have little chance of advancement for themselves, once they are set in manual working-class jobs without special educational qualifications to help them up. There are many imponderables here, as about other features of working-class consciousness today and tomorrow. But there is certainly no guarantee of a contribution to social order from the routinization of social mobility through education. The effects could well be the other way.

J. Westergaard and H. Resler, *Class in a Capitalist Society*, 1976, pp. 340–2.

Questions

1. *Assess the evidence provided by Westergaard and Resler on family background and patterns of mobility.*
2. *Does the educational system provide the main avenue of social mobility in contemporary Britain? Give reasons for your answer.*
3. *Westergaard and Resler provide a number of speculative comments about educational opportunity and social mobility. Outline and discuss the kinds of questions that sociologists need to ask in order to provide evidence on the implications of education and social mobility in contemporary Britain.*

ESSAY QUESTIONS

1. 'The educational system is alleged to provide a ladder of opportunity but in practice, it merely reinforces the status quo.' Discuss. (AEB, 1981)
2. 'Education promotes social mobility.' 'Education simply reinforces existing patterns of social class, race and sexual stratification.' Assess

the relative merits of these two contrasting claims. (JMB, 1981)
3. Describe the major trends in the rate of social mobility since 1945. What are the major factors determining rates of social mobility? (Oxford, 1983)
4. Has Britain become a more 'open' society since 1945?

FURTHER READING

1. T. Blackstone, 'Falling short of meritocracy', *The Times Higher Education Supplement*, 18 January 1980, p. 14.

   A comprehensive review of *Origins and Destinations* which relates it to previous studies, summarises the research and raises questions that can be used in evaluating the study.

2. A. H. Halsey, *Change in British Society*, Oxford University Press, 1978.

   A set of very readable essays that were originally given as Reith lectures. Contains useful material on social class, social mobility and education.

3. A. F. Heath, *Social Mobility*, Fontana, 1981.

   A very readable commentary on the data relating to debates about social mobility. It contains a good index to help locate educational issues.

4. J. Karabel and A. H. Halsey (eds), *Power and Ideology in Education*, Oxford University Press, 1977.

   The introduction to this collection contains a synthesis of British and American research on social class and social mobility in relation to education. The papers may be used selectively.

5. F. Musgrove, *School and the Social Order*, Wiley, 1979.

   Offers a critique of much research in the sociology of education including work on educational opportunity, equality and social mobility (see Ch. 6).

6. J. Purvis and M. Hales (eds), *Achievement and Inequality in Education*, Routledge and Kegan Paul, 1983.

   A useful collection of essays – see especially part four on education and qualifications. It also includes Payne (1980).

7. P. Robinson, *Perspectives on the Sociology of Education: An Introduction*, Routledge and Kegan Paul, 1981.

   Contains a useful chapter that summarises current debates on educational opportunity (see Ch. 9).

8. H. Silver (ed), *Equal Opportunity in Education*, Methuen, 1973.

   An excellent collection of papers linked by a very good set of editorial commentaries to guide the reader through this debate.

9. W. Tyler, *The Sociology of Educational Inequality*, Methuen, 1977.

   A concise, readable survey of the major debates on educational inequality. The author favours Boudon's model of mobility and opportunity.

10. J. Westergaard and H. Resler, *Class in a Capitalist Society*, Harmondsworth, Penguin, 1976.

A Maxist perspective on class inequality in Britain. Part four on inequalities of opportunity looks at social mobility, educational opportunity and the significance of the trends.

4

Patterns and processes of educational achievement

The relationship between social class and educational attainment has been a common area of research for British sociologists. Much of this work has been concerned with the operation of the tripartite system of secondary education and with who succeeded and who failed to gain entry to grammar schools. One of the key problems for sociologists was how to explain the broad differences that exist in educational attainment between different social classes. In addressing this issue, different theories have been advanced to account for the class differentials in educational achievement:

First, *the differential ability theory* which maintains that class differences in attainment can be explained by academic ability. However, such a theory raises questions about the basis of assessing intelligence and explaining class differences in measured intelligence which leads into the nature/nurture, hereditary/environment debate (cf. Lee and Newby, 1983, pp. 86–99).

Secondly, *the differential access* theory which was particularly relevant when selection examinations were widely in operation as it was believed that the provision of secondary education for all would lead to an increase in working-class pupils in some schools. Such a theory could also be used to consider the position of independent schools in the English educational system and the access which boys and girls get to study particular subjects (especially science) in schools (cf. Kelly, 1981).

Thirdly, *the differential education provision theory* which proposes that social class differences in educational achievement is a consequence of the fact that the middle class get a 'better' education than the working class. It is this question of educational provision that has been taken up not only with reference to social classes, but also in relation to mixed and single-sex schools (Byrne, 1975) and to the resources provided by different education authorities (see the last reading in this chapter).

Fourthly, *the cultural discontinuity theory* which suggests that education is concerned with the transmission of the culture

73

of the dominant group and hence favours the middle class; a position adopted by Bourdieu. This theory may also include the differential access and differential provision theories and helps to explain social class differences in education. Questions concerning this theory have focused on the family, socialisation, language and social class.

All these theories have had some impact upon educational research and educational policy, as the evidence is far from clear cut.

Although social class has been used as a key variable in research on inequality in general and education in particular, many researchers and commentators have pointed to the importance of gender and race as variables that can be used to examine educational achievement. This allows questions to be posed about patterns of success and failure between social classes and about differential achievement between boys and girls and between different ethnic groups.

The first three readings in this chapter focus on statistical data. We begin by looking at the pattern of educational achievement among men in different social classes, in England and Wales, among boys and girls in Great Britain and among different ethnic groups in six local education authorities in England. Many studies have highlighted the importance of secondary school examinations for pupils and it is the task of the sociologist to explain why particular groups succeed while others fail in public examinations.

There is a range of material and cultural factors that have been used to explain the different patterns of achievement. We begin by looking at the findings provided by Douglas's longitudinal study of school pupils which in turn have been confirmed by the National Child Development Study. In these accounts it is the family and family size related to social class that is said to result in different patterns of achievement. However, it is difficult for sociologists to be able to specify what constitutes family background. For some sociologists it is patterns of socialisation that give advantages to some pupils rather than others. Meanwhile, Pierre Bourdieu has discussed the way in which the family is a source of 'cultural capital' that results in advantages for pupils from families that transmit the cultural pattern which is followed in the school.

A further important area of study concerns the relationship between language and education. In England it is Basil Bernstein who has discussed the relationship between social class, language use and school achievement. However, this work is far from clear cut as questions have been raised by numerous commentators about the explanations provided by Bernstein and by Labov on children's use of language. A major criticism of Bernstein's work relates to his use of social class and the way it influences patterns of communication and socialisation.

It is not only the concept of class that has been questioned by sociologists. Questions can also be asked about what constitutes 'ability', 'attainment' and 'achievement' (cf. Beck *et al.*, 1976; especially part 3). In this connection, Walden and Walkerdine question the way in which the differential attainment of boys and girls has been explained.

Finally, the reading from Byrne, Williamson and Fletcher's work helps us to recall that the social factors which contribute to educational performance are not merely attributes of individuals but are also related to the practices and policies of local education authorities. They argue that schools do make a difference to pupil performance; a point that underlines the importance of some of the processes identified in the following chapters which will influence patterns of educational attainment.

SOCIAL CLASS AND SCHOOL EXAMINATIONS

Although the study *Origins and Destinations* (1980) concentrates only on the social origins and educational destinations of men, it does provide recent data on patterns of educational achievement for a representative sample of the male population in England and Wales. The following table summarises data on social class and school examinations.

Reading 1

Table. Social Class and School Examinations

Father's social class	Percentage staying on until 16 or later	Percentage obtaining school certificate or 1 or more O-levels	Column 2 as a proportion of column 1 (O-level success rate)	Percentage staying on until 18 or or later	Percentage obtaining higher school certificate or 1 or more A-levels	Column 5 as a proportion of column 4 (A-level success rate)
I, II (N=1072)	70.0	58.1	0.83	28.2	26.9	0.93
III, IV, V (N=2475)	32.6	24.2	0.74	7.7	6.9	0.90
VI, VII, VIII (N=4482)	26.8	11.8	0.71	3.0	2.8	0.93

Note: The classes are defined as follows:

over

I	Higher grade professionals, administrators, managers and proprietors	The
II	Lower grade professionals, administrators and managers. Supervisors and higher grade technicians	Service Class
III	Clerical, sales and rank-and-file service workers	
IV	Small proprietors and self-employed artisans. The 'petty bourgeoisie'	The Intermediate
V	Lower grade technicians and foremen. The aristocracy of labour	Class
VI	Semi-skilled manual workers in industry	The
VII	Semi- and unskilled manual workers in industry	Working
VIII	Agricultural workers and smallholders	Class

A. H. Halsey, A. F. Heath and J. M. Ridge, *Origins and Destinations*, 1980, based on Table 8.12, p. 142.

Questions

1. *Describe the relationship between social class and pupils staying on at school until (i) sixteen or later (ii) eighteen or later. How would you account for these relationships?*
2. *Is there a relationship between social class and examination performance? Give reasons for your answer.*
3. *Do working-class pupils who remain at school have a similar chance of examination success as middle-class pupils? Give reasons for your answer.*
4. *How would you account for the trends shown in this table?*

THE EXAMINATION PERFORMANCE OF GIRLS AND BOYS IN ENGLAND AND WALES

There is a wealth of educational statistics produced each year by such bodies as the Department of Education and Science and the Office of Population, Censuses and Surveys. While these data may summarise trends they cannot 'speak for themselves' but require analysis. It is the sociologist's task to account for the trends that are shown in educational data such as those provided in the chart opposite.

Reading 2

Questions

1. *Use the chart opposite to describe the main trends in examination performance between boys and girls.*
2. *How would you account for the different patterns of achievement in (i) physics (ii) biology?*

3. *Outline and discuss the questions that you would pose in an investigation to find out why so few girls passed physics.*

Chart. School leavers – GCE 'O' level Grades A–C Passes in Selected Subjects by Sex 1970/71 and 1981/82

England & Wales

School leavers possessing an 'O' level pass[1] grade A–C in these subjects

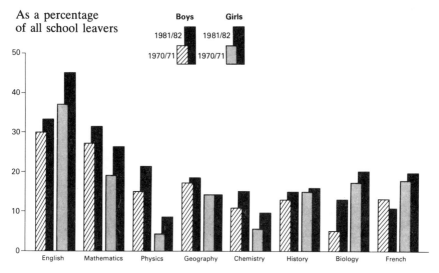

[1] Including grade 1 results in CSE examinations, but excluding 'O' level passes on 'A' level papers.

Social Trends 1984, 1983, chart 3.7, p. 47.

RACE AND EDUCATIONAL ACHIEVEMENT

There has been a range of studies conducted in the United Kingdom on the educational attainment of black pupils in schools. These investigations have been summarised by Tomlinson (1983) and include case studies of schools and large-scale surveys. One of the most recent studies was commissioned by the Rampton Committee (1981) who focused on West Indian pupils in six local education authorities in England.

Reading 3

Table. CSE, 'O' Level and 'A' Level Achievements among School-leavers in Six Local Education Authorities in England

	Asians	West Indians	All other leavers	All maintained school leavers in England (%)
		Leavers in 6 LEAs		
	%	%	%	
CSE and 'O' level				
No graded results (includes those not attempting examinations)	19	17	22	14
At least 1 graded result but less than 5 higher grades	63	81	62	66
5 or more higher grades	18	3	16	21
'A' level				
No 'A' level pass	87	98	88	87
One or more 'A' level pass	13	2	12	13
Total (number)	527	799	4,852	693,840

Rampton Committee, *West Indian Children in Our Schools*, 1981, Tables C and D, p. 8.

Questions
1. *Summarise the data provided in the table.*
2. *Offer one hypothesis about the distribution of examination passes among different ethnic groups.*
3. *Discuss what further data you would wish to collect to cast light on your hypothesis.*

SOCIAL CLASS, FAMILY AND EDUCATION
Among the best-known studies in the sociology of education is J.

W. B. Douglas's longitudinal investigation of 5,386 children born in March 1946. Although published in the 1960s, its evidence on the waste of ability and talent has influenced educational debate and educational policy over many years. Similar findings have been produced in a further longitudinal study reported in Fogelman (1983)

Reading 4

Educational Opportunity

The social class differences in educational opportunity which were considerable at the primary school stage have increased at the secondary and extend now even to pupils of high ability. Thus nearly half the lower manual working class pupils of high ability have left school before they are sixteen and a half years.

Early leaving and low job aspirations make it probable that as many as 5 per cent of the next generation of manual workers will be recruited from pupils who, in other circumstances, might have qualified for administrative or professional occupations.

The manual working class pupils, compared with those of the middle class, are least handicapped when they are in the best staffed and best equipped schools and in those areas of the country which have the largest proportion of selective school places.

An analysis of the length of school life among the lower manual working class pupils of borderline ability and above shows that both parental interest and school staffing and equipment are associated with age of leaving. These two factors are of course highly correlated, but neither adequately compensates for the deficiency of the other – the interest of the parents alone is insufficient to counter the deficiencies of the schools.

Independent Schools

The pupils at the boys' public schools, once their ability and the circumstances of their families are taken into account are no more successful, as judged by 'O' level results and age of leaving up to sixteen and a half years, than grammar school pupils. The pupils at other independent schools (i.e. those outside the Headmasters' Conference) are considerably less successful.

The pupils at independent girls' schools are considerably less successful than those at grammar schools. They leave earlier and have less good 'O' level results, whether the schools are members of the Headmistresses' Association or not.

Educational Progress of Boys and Girls

The test scores of the girls, on the average, fall below those of the boys between the ages of eleven and fifteen – with the one exception of the verbal intelligence test. Their disadvantage in each social class is greatest in mathematics. Girls on the whole are less likely to get good 'O' level certificates than boys but once allowances are made for their lower measured ability at fifteen, their 'O' level results are no worse than the boys' and indeed at lower levels of ability are rather better.

In co-educational schools, the average fifteen year test performance of the boys and girls is similar and even in mathematics the girls are not significantly below the boys. At co-educational grammar schools the early maturing girls stay on as long or longer than late maturing girls, whereas at single sex grammar schools they leave earlier.

Education North and South of the Border

Scottish pupils at each age make lower scores in non-verbal tests than the English and Welsh. In reading, the Scots are ahead at eight but not later, and in arithmetic and mathematics they have a persisting lead over those south of the border. Rather more Scottish pupils leave at the earliest opportunity but the proportions staying on to the beginning of the 1962/3 session and the proportions gaining 'O' level passes are similar in the two countries. A higher percentage of Scottish than English and Welsh boys expect to enter higher education.

Parental Influences

The attitudes of the parents to the education of their children changed little over the period covered by this study.

Parents of widely different ages have similar educational aspirations for their children and it seems that they adopt current attitudes towards education rather than carry forward those of their own generation.

The interest and encouragement that parents give their children is closely linked to their own educational history. Any attempt that the parents made to secure for themselves education beyond the elementary school level, even if this was not successfully completed, is associated with higher aspirations for their own children's educational success.

Insecurity in a family, whether from father's absence,

unemployment, illness or death is associated with poorer performance at school and early leaving. It is prolonged insecurity that seems to be important; the sudden death of a father, whether early or late in the life of his child, has no apparent effect on school work.

Family Structure

Children from large families make low scores in all attainment tests at all ages. There is however no evidence of an increasing educational handicap at secondary school, indeed in the manual working class there is rather less difference in the attainment of children from large and small families at fifteen, than there was when they were first tested at eight.

The more young children there are in the family when a child is learning to talk the lower his score in the eight year old vocabulary test. This early deficiency in the understanding of words is not made up later.

Pupils from large families leave school earlier than expected at each level of measured ability. Financial reasons alone are insufficient to explain this for the youngest in large families also leave early, even though there are likely to be fewer calls on the family income than when their elder brothers and sisters were the same age.

First-born boys in families of 2 or 3 make higher scores in the attainment tests and are academically more successful and more aspiring than their younger brothers and sisters. They are also superior in attainment to only children. For the girls this difference is not found.

Pupils from two-child families with birth intervals of 2 to 4 years make higher scores in all tests than those with either shorter or longer intervals, they get superior 'O' level results and leave school later. This holds for both older and younger boys and girls: the advantage of those with 2 to 4 year intervals being as great at eight as later.

J. W. B. Douglas, J. M. Ross and H. R. Simpson, *All Our Future*, 1971, pp. 196–200.

Questions

1. *What patterns emerge from Douglas's study concerning: (i) social class and education; (ii) gender and education.*
2. *Explain how (i) parents and (ii) family structures influence educational attainment.*

3. *Assess the relative importance of social class, gender and the family on educational achievement. What other social factors would you want to consider? Give reasons for your answer.*

CULTURAL CAPITAL

In the 1970s and 1980s, the work of Pierre Bourdieu made a considerable impact on the sociology of education. Using evidence from France, Bourdieu argued that education demanded a linguistic and cultural competence which resulted in an advantage to pupils whose families could transmit those elements of culture that are required for success in schools.

Reading 5

Pierre Bourdieu's concern with education and social stratification is rather different; as he puts it:

> . . . the controlled mobility of a limited category of individuals, carefully selected and modified by and for individual ascent, is not incompatible with the permanence of structures, and . . . it is even capable of contributing to social stability in the only way conceivable in societies based upon democratic ideals and thereby may help to perpetuate the structure of class relations.

It is to this continuity (or reproduction) of a class society that he directs his attention. He points out that the educational system (in this case in France but the same would apply to England, or to Scotland) . . . demands a linguistic and cultural competence that it does not itself provide. This gives an advantage to those from families that diffusely and implicitly transmit the necessary 'instruments of appropriation of culture'. As a wealth of statistics show, an apparently open and meritocratic system is therefore predisposed to favour those who already have '*cultural capital*'. Possession of cultural capital is closely associated with possession of economic capital; Bourdieu's detailed examination of the French upper classes demonstrates, however, that the relationship between the two forms is complex: the distribution is not the same; cultural capital (i.e. academic qualifications) is most effective (outside the academic market) when combined with economic capital and political power; and in any case those with economic capital both have more chances of possessing cultural capital *and* are more able to do without it. Thus there is value in considering cultural capital and its reproduction separately.

R. K. Brown, 'Introduction', in R. K. Brown (ed), *Knowledge, Education and Cultural Change*, 1973, p. 5.

Questions
1. *What do you think would be covered by the term 'cultural capital'?*
2. *What statistical data would you need to see the way in which the educational system favours those with cultural capital?*
3. *How far do you think Bourdieu's ideas are relevant to the English school system? Illustrate your answer with examples.*

SOCIAL CLASS, LANGUAGE AND EDUCATION

Among the mosst distinguished contributors to the sociology of education is Basil Bernstein who has worked on the study of language. Since the early 1960s, Bernstein has been developing, extending and elaborating his accounts especially in response to commentaries and critical accounts. Some of his major papers are provided in the volume *Class Codes and Control Volume I (CCC 1)* (1971). Bernstein's position in the 1970s is summarised by Stubbs who also presents an evaluation of the work.

Reading 6

In order to discover whether someone is an elaborated or restricted-code user, one has to look at the language he or she uses in what Bernstein calls the four critical socializing contexts (*CCC 1*, p. 206): *regulative*, e.g. being told off by mother; *instructional*, e.g. the classroom; *imaginative*, e.g. in play; and *interpersonal*, e.g. in talk with others where the child is made aware of emotional states. If the linguistic realizations of these four contexts are 'predominantly' in terms of restricted speech variants, then the deep structure of the communication is said to be a restricted code. Conversely for elaborated code.

Note one most important point which has caused much confusion. Codes are *defined* as abstract, underlying principles which regulate communication and generate speech. People do not speak codes, just as they do not speak grammar: both grammar and codes are abstract, underlying systems. It is therefore incoherent to refer to a child as a 'restricted-code speaker'. One can only talk of a child who tends to use restricted speech variants in certain contexts.

Bernstein further adds to the complexity of the theory by distinguishing two *family types* (p. 209). In *positional* families, there is said to be clear-cut definition of the status of different members of the family, as 'father', 'grandmother' and so on. In *person-centred* families these status distinctions are blurred in favour of members' unique characteristics. Bernstein claims, without giving any details, that the communication structure in these different family types is differently focused, such that we should expect restricted code in positional families and elaborated code in person-centred families (p. 211). He claims that both family types can be found in both MC and WC, but implies that, at the present time, positional families are more characteristic of the WC.

What has Bernstein now said? What is the form of his theory? He is attempting to formulate a theory which relates a child's social class, family background, language use and cognitive style. He still claims (*CCC 1*, p. 209) that access to the codes is 'broadly related to social class' and that there 'may well be selective access to elaborated code' (p. 208); that is, some WC speakers do not have access to elaborated code but most (?) MC speakers have access to both. This is because (so runs his argument) there is selective access to the role systems which evoke the use of the codes (p. 208). Within positional families we should 'expect' restricted code (p. 211). But both positional and person-centred families are found in both WC and MC (p. 209). Finally, to know if a given piece of language realizes restricted or elaborated code, we should have to observe the language use across the four critical socializing contexts – for an elaborated speech variant (defined in terms of meanings, not observable linguistic forms) may realize a restricted code, and vice versa.

From the way I have summarized this position, it will be clear that I believe the theory is now formulated in such a way that no testable claim is now being made. The model apparently being proposed might be summarised [as shown at the top of p. 85]. The arrows represent links between levels. The vertical columns represent 'expected' links. Thus WC families may be expected to be positional, but they may be person-centred. A positional family would lead one to expect code restriction, but if it should show (unspecified) signs of being person-centred, then the children might be able to switch codes.

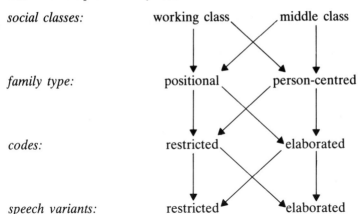

social classes: working class   middle class

family type: positional   person-centred

codes: restricted   elaborated

speech variants: restricted   elaborated

When the theory is set out in this way, it becomes clear that it is not a real theory. No real predictions are made, for example, about which forms of family are related to which codes. All we have are 'expectations', unsupported by evidence. More important, it is not possible to refute such a theory from empirical evidence and observations. Genuine scientific theories make predictions that certain things (X) will happen under certain conditions, and that other things (Y) will not happen. The statement may involve specifying a statistical probability that X will occur: that is, a definable margin of error may be specified in the prediction. If Y does happen, the theory must be altered or abandoned, since it does not fit the facts. But Bernstein's model sets no real constraints on what may happen. An example of an elaborated speech variant may be expected to be a realization of elaborated code, but it may realize restricted code too. We can only know which code it realizes by investigating whether the critical socializing contexts of the speaker were predominantly characterized by restricted or elaborated speech variants – but this is uninvestigable.

Gordon (1981, p. 81) has made the following valiant attempt to give a succinct statement of what Bernstein has actually claimed in two papers published in 1970 and 1971:

> social class → family structure → roles → modes of early socialization → roles . . . modes of perception . . . access to codes → codes → speech → educational attainment

An arrow indicates a claimed causal link; the dots indicate a link which is irremediably obscure in Bernstein's writings. Gordon notes that 'roles' occurs twice, and that the whole chain of causality is particularly obscure after the second occurrence. He notes also that the first and last entities in the chain are simply taken for granted.

The lack of linguistic analysis in Benstein's work

The major limitation in Bernstein's work, from the point of view of its ability to make precise and testable statements, is the *almost total lack of linguistic exemplification* of his theories. Most of the papers are entirely abstract speculations with no precise linguistic data. Where Bernstein does provide brief linguistic examples and data, this is either (a) invented, i.e. imagined, fictional anecdotes (e.g. *CCC 1*, p. 201), or (b) hypothetical, e.g. mothers were asked what they would say *if* their child was naughty, or (c) taken from experimental test situations, as in Hawkins's experiment. There are no extended real-life examples of language use anywhere in Bernstein's papers: no more than a couple of conversational fragments in footnotes (e.g. *CCC 1*, p. 283), and no examples whatsoever of actual language use between mothers and children in the home or between teachers and pupils in the classroom.

M. Stubbs, *Language, Schools and Classrooms*, 1983, pp. 59–61.

Questions
1. *What does Bernstein claim is the relationship between social class, family and language codes?*
2. *Evaluate Gordon's summary of Bernstein's work on social class, family, language and educational attainment.*
3. *Do you think Bernstein's work constitutes a theory? Give reasons for your answer.*

THE EDUCATIONAL PERFORMANCE OF GIRLS AND BOYS: THE CASE OF MATHEMATICS

Much of the research on educational achievement has focused on social class with the result that the differential performance of boys and girls has been overlooked. However, much recent research is no longer gender blind, as writers have begun to question explanations concerning the educational performance of girls and boys.

Reading 7

In our experience the early good performance of girls tends to be
explained away as unimportant or insignificant. We have often
heard girls' early achievements attributed to *just*, *simply* or *only*
something or other. The very use of these terms is an immediate
devaluation. The most common uses of the 'only' are 'they're
only good at computation', 'they only follow the rules, they don't
have proper mathematical concepts' and other similar explanations. These explanations amount to virtually the same thing:
they assert that the girls' performance is based on precisely that
kind of understanding which tends to be the bane of primary
school teachers' lives: rote learning or 'computational techniques'
rather than 'real understanding', 'knowing *how*' rather than
'knowing *that*', 'procedural' rather than 'propositional' knowledge. This explanation devalues the actual performance of girls
and suggests that it is not based on the same intellectual
foundations as that of the boys.

The type of mathematics at which boys achieve good results in
the secondary school is held to be more intellectually advanced
than the 'low-level' mathematics at which girls do well. A
consequence is that boys' performances are valued the more
highly. Writers explain away the educational performance of girls
at this age in different ways. Yates and Pidgeon (1957), for
instance, discussing the differences in the 11-plus scores of girls
and boys, attributed the performance of girls to physical
maturation. Because girls grow physically faster than boys and
reach puberty earlier this was considered a cause of their early
high performance. In effect, this tells us very little since it is a
moot point as to whether physical and intellectual characteristics
can be measured in the same terms, and indeed whether there is
or can be a direct relationship between physical and intellectual
maturation. Yet, it was on this basis that different 11-plus pass
marks used to be allocated. In the view of Yates and Pidgeon this
was the 'fairest' method they could devise, since:

> If the pass marks are made equivalent for the two sexes the
> number of girls admitted to grammar schools will in most
> areas substantially exceed the number of boys. In view of the
> fact therefore that these differences exist at the age of eleven
> and that there is considerable uncertainty as to when and to
> what extent they eventually disappear the most satisfactory
> course . . . to adopt would seem to be to treat boys and girls

separately for the purpose of allocation to secondary school (p. 168–9)

In our view, these 'differences' do not 'disappear', rather the good performance of girls is explained away or devalued because it does not conform to a stereotype.

Girls tend to see mathematics and the sciences as 'hard', intellect-based, complex and masculine (Weinreich-Haste, 1979). The eulogy of Hermann Weyl at the grave of Emmy Noether (one of the most famous of all mathematicians) sums up several popular notions about the female who is good at mathematics.

> No one could contend that the Graces had stood by her cradle, but if we in Gottingen referred to her as 'der Noether' (masculine article), it was also done with a respectful recognition of her power as a creative thinker who *seemed to have broken through the barrier of sex.* (our italics)

As we can see from this extract Weyl encompasses the popular views that being good at mathematics and being attractive and feminine are incompatible, and that being female is a constraint on ability to be a creative thinker. If adolescent girls see mathematics as somehow inappropriate and 'masculine' it is in no way surprising. Girls appear to be in a 'no-win', 'catch 22' situation. If they fail at mathematics they lack true intellect but are truly female. If they succeed they are only able to do so by following rules and if they conquer that hurdle they become somehow less than female. Boys are not so susceptible to such pejoratives: their successes are 'real' and their failures 'under-achievement' and thus susceptible to amelioration. The perform-ance of boys is taken as the standard and girls are judged in relation to it.

R. Walden and V. Walkerdine, *Girls and Mathematics: the Early Years*, *Bedford Way Papers No. 8*, 1982, pp. 61–3.

Questions
1. *Compare and contrast the explanations provided in this reading for the educational performance of girls and boys in mathematics.*
2. *What sociological concepts would you use to analyse the educational performance of girls and boys? Give reasons for using the concepts you select.*
3. *Is educational achievement socially constructed? Give reasons for your answer.*

EDUCATIONAL RESOURCES AND EDUCATIONAL ATTAINMENT

Much work on the social factors involved in educability has personalised educational success and failure. Byrne, Williamson and Fletcher examined the different rates of educational attainment of children from different social classes which, they argue, can be explained by the differences in the kinds and quality of educational resources available to them.

Reading 8

The kind of policy a local authority pursues influences the extent and character of what it provides. This provision, in turn, is related to measures of educational attainment. Where provision is high there is a tendency for attainment to be high. Seen from this perspective, high levels of provision can be thought of as influencing the demand for education. Certainly, when provision and environmental measures are taken into account, the importance of class-background variables by themselves is reduced significantly.

We have not attempted to examine the precise mechanisms involved in the relationship between provision and attainment for it would be almost impossible to do, given the data base for this part of our study. Nonetheless, our results so far suggest that the level of educational provision in local authority areas has a very direct bearing on educational life chances of children in those areas. In this respect, our results run counter to some recent research reports, in particular the Coleman Report in the United States. For reasons which we have already set out, it is difficult to compare our results directly with other research findings. The whole tenor of much educational discussion since Coleman has been dominated by a suspicion that schools and what they provide make little difference to the educational achievement of schoolchildren. As Hodgson summarised the Coleman report, reviewing the way in which the report was received in the United States:

> When other things were equal, the report said, factors such as the amount of money spent per pupil, or the number of books in the library, or physical facilities such as gymnasiums or cafeterias or laboratories, or even differences in the curriculum, seemed to make no appreciable differences to the childrens' level of achievement. (Hodgson, 1973, p. 356)

Our results suggest a different conclusion. When education and *environment* are equal, the influence of class background on the attainment of children in different LEA areas is markedly reduced. Such equality, of course, is rarely if ever found in practice. The argument therefore is about the mode of influence of class background upon educational attainment. Our results lead to the suggestion that the most important mode is through the structure of educational provision. In short, schools *do* matter.

D. Byrne, B. Williamson and B. Fletcher, *The Poverty of Education: A Study in the Politics of Opportunity*, 1975, pp. 165–6.

Questions
1. *Outline the main findings in the authors' research.*
2. *Discuss the ways in which educational resources can contribute to educational attainment.*
3. *To what extent can education and the 'environment' (para. 3) reduce the influence of social class on educational achievement? Give examples to illustrate your answer.*

ESSAY QUESTIONS
1. Examine sociological explanations of differences in educational achievement between EITHER a) genders OR b) ethnic groups. (AEB, 1982)
2. Is there a relationship between 'linguistic codes' and educational achievement?
3. Consider the view that differential educational achievement is primarily a way of legitimating social inequality. (London, 1982)
4. Discuss the relationship between social background and educational achievement.

FURTHER READING
There is a vast literature on social class, gender and race in relation to patterns of inequality, achievement and under-achievement in education. Accordingly, this list provides only a brief guide to a range of sources that review different aspects of this field of study.

1. B. Bernstein, *Class Codes and Control Volume I*, Routledge and Kegan Paul, 1971.
   Provides all the major papers that Bernstein has written on language and class together with a commentary by the author. In subsequent

editions further revisions have been made and additional papers are available in a third volume with the same title (Bernstein, 1975).

2. R. G. Burgess, 'Patterns and processes of education in the United Kingdom', in P. Abrams and R. K. Brown (eds), *UK Society Today: Work, Urbanism and Inequality*, 2nd edn, Weidenfeld and Nicolson, 1984.

   Provides a review of trends in the various sectors of the state education systems of England and Wales, Scotland and Northern Ireland (the independent sector is reviewed in the same volume by Stanworth, 1984). In particular, class, gender and race are considered in relation to educational attainment.

3. A. D. Edwards, *Language in Culture and Class*, Heinemann, 1976.

   A survey of the literature. Chapter 4 reviews language and achievement.

4. M. Fuller, *Inequality: Class, Gender and Race* (Block 6. Unit 27 of Open University Course E205 Conflict and Change in Education) Open University Press, 1984.

   Includes a review of major concepts, trends and debates on race and educational achievement. It is very clearly written.

5. A. H. Halsey, A. F. Heath and J. M. Ridge, *Origins and Destinations: Family, Class and Education in Modern Britain*, Oxford University Press, 1980.

   The most recent study that provides data on educational achievement in England and Wales, although only of a male sample.

6. J. Purvis and M. Hales (eds), *Achievement and Inequality in Education*, Routledge and Kegan Paul, 1983.

   Provides readings grouped around teachers' perspectives, pupils' perspectives, sexual inequalities and educational provision, and education and qualifications.

7. I. Reid, *Social Class Differences in Britain*, 2nd edn, Grant McIntyre, 1981.

   Chapter 6 provides a good review of the literature on social class and education.

8. S. Sharpe, *'Just Like a Girl'*, Penguin, 1976.

   Chapter 4 on contradictions in female education is particularly helpful.

9. M. Stubbs, *Language, Schools and Classrooms*, 2nd edn, Methuen, 1983.

   An excellent review of the literature with complete chapters assessing the work of Bernstein and Labov.

10. S. Tomlinson, *Ethnic Minorities in British Schools: A Review of the Literature, 1960–82*, Heinemann, 1983.

    Contains two chapters that assess the educational performance of West Indian and Asian pupils.

5

The sociology of school organisation

School assembly, timetables, streaming, mixed ability grouping and pastoral care are all parts of school organisation; they are all aspects of the everyday world of schooling with which most people are familiar. Yet despite their familiarity, sociologists have done relatively little to explain and understand the processes associated with school organisation.

At one time the school was for sociologists little more than a 'black box' in which pupils were processed. Sociologists tended to leave school organisation unquestioned so that something was known about school input and output but relatively little about what went on within the school itself. From the end of the 1960s, British sociologists began to examine the school through individual case studies. To begin with, the focus was on secondary education, but by the 1970s, sociologists could be found in comprehensive schools, and primary as well as secondary schools. In addition, surveys of schools in the state and independent sectors were also conducted.

Among the questions posed about school organisation were: how do secondary schools organise the activities of their pupils? To what extent does school organisation influence the achievement of the pupils? Certainly, it is questions about the effects of school structure upon academic ability that have most often been examined and have been at the centre of debates. Yet we still lack a systematic analysis of the way in which various aspects of schooling influence pupil behaviour and pupil performance.

The readings selected for this chapter begin by addressing certain aspects of school organisation that are in danger of being taken for granted. First, we turn to school assembly and school rules to see the way in which they are used by teachers to transmit messages about schools and schooling. Secondly, we look at the way in which ritual in school can be used to create consensus and differentiate between groups of pupils. Here, we have a review of Basil Bernstein's work as he has also contributed to this area of study.

In the third and fourth readings we examine the ways in which schools differentiate pupils. First, we turn to David Hargreaves' work in a boys' secondary modern school to examine the relationship between peer group subculture and the formal organisation of the school reflected in the streaming process. A similar theme is also taken up by Colin Lacey who discusses the way in which differentiation by teachers is related to polarisation among pupil groups in a grammar school. While these two studies discuss fundamental processes that occur among pupils, we should note that they have only examined boys' schools and schools that were organised within the tripartite system of secondary education. Accordingly, we need to consider the extent to which these processes might still apply in girls' schools, in coeducational schools and in comprehensive schools.

To some extent this has been done in Stephen Ball's *Beachside Comprehensive* (1981) which uses some of the concepts developed in Lacey's analysis to examine banding and mixed ability grouping in a school. Ball's work is placed alongside a survey of mixed ability grouping in Banbury School by David Newbold. These two studies have been conducted in different ways as Newbold's work is predominantly based on survey research, while Stephen Ball used an observational approach to study Beachside. The conclusions that they arrive at concerning mixed ability grouping are somewhat different and contribute to the ongoing debate about the internal organisation of comprehensive schools. This evidence needs to be evaluated, if we are to assess the strengths and weaknesses of the arguments.

One of the main questions that has been raised in the popular debate about comprehensive education is the extent to which school processes and school organisation have an effect on pupils. A key study in this area has been the work of Michael Rutter and his associates who looked at twelve secondary schools within Inner London. Although this study is said to lack 'theory', it has, nevertheless, provided a 'message' for the popular debate on schooling. In order to get some flavour of the debate that surrounded the reception of this evidence, the final reading is taken from a review of the Rutter research. Again, it is important to assess the evidence before deciding which side to take.

In turn, we may also identify gaps in the literature on school organisation. For example, all the readings in this chapter are taken from studies of state secondary schools which reflects the dominant thrust of sociological study. We need more studies of primary schools, state schools and independent schools if we are to reach a detailed understanding of the processes that occur within the English school system. Nevertheless, some sociologists are beginning to broaden our understanding of the schooling process by examining classrooms and specific curricula. These are considered in the next two chapters and should be read alongside this material.

INTRODUCING SCHOOL ORGANISATION

Assemblies, school rules and the timetable are all important aspects of school routine that can be examined by sociologists. It is the way in which these aspects of school culture are transmitted to pupils that is the subject of this reading in which a headmaster presents school organisation to his pupils.

Reading 1

Several school assemblies were devoted to school organization. This was particularly prevalent in assemblies that were taken by the headmaster in the early part of the autumn term 1973. In these assemblies he talked to the new pupils who had come from small junior schools in the city. As these schools were only three hundred strong and subdivided into ten classes, large schools of over one thousand pupils subdivided into houses, tutorials, mixed-ability groups and sets were unknown to them. So it was essential to describe the school structure and explain how it worked. In one assembly I made the following record of Mr Goddard's talk:

> The headmaster began his talk by telling the pupils that they might all come from different schools but they did come from the same area of the city and therefore the idea behind McGregor School was to bring them altogether. He remarked that the school was divided into houses. However, he added, Westminster and Arundel were not enemies as they could look at each other and see how they were alike. He said that their similarities were based on the uniform. He added, 'It's no good to go home and say, "Nobody wears the uniform" because most people do wear it'. He explained that there were people who did not wear some of the uniform but they would probably have a good reason for it and their tutor or their head of house would probably know about it. He told them that in the past the school had had several problems with bullies but when people had told him about it he had sorted it out and cut those bullies down to size. He said that he had done this in the past and that he would do it again . . . Finally he said the the school was like a family. 'We are all part of a family – the family of the school, the family of God and the family of man.'

This assembly is illustrative of the way in which the headmaster presented the school to new pupils. He introduced the idea of a large comprehensive school by explaining the way in which McGregor drew together pupils from different Catholic schools in the area. However, he also explained the way in which large numbers of pupils were grouped together into smaller identifiable groups called houses. Here, the way in which the house system sub-divided the school and its pupils was not mentioned. Indeed, Goddard emphasized *consensus* between houses. Finally, he drew an analogy between the houses and a family where all individuals were known. While talking about the houses Mr Goddard also introduced the house staff with whom he thought the pupils should be in close contact. He also illustrated the values and norms held by members of the school by discussing bullying as an activity which would not be tolerated at McGregor.

Shortly after this assembly, Mr Goddard issued a written notice which was displayed in all houses and classrooms and stated:

SOME POINTS OF PRACTICE FOR ALL PUPILS

1 All are expected to be at the correct place at the correct time.
2 All are to conduct themselves sensibly and to show consideration for others at all times.
3 All items of clothing and articles brought to school must be marked with the owner's name and either the house initial or the house colour.
4 All are to treat both buildings and school equipment, furniture and books with care and respect.
5 Movement about the site should be purposeful, conducted at a reasonable walking pace and always display courtesy and care for others. In general a keep left policy is used whenever there is congestion.
6 Pupils are expected to conform to the school code governing appearance and for each this is interpreted by the head of house.
7 All are expected to treat everyone with respect and courtesy.
8 All are expected to keep the school tidy.
9 All instructions from teachers and other adults are to be obeyed.
10 All are to refrain from prohibited practices.

At the same time these notes were issued to the pupils, some explanatory notes were also provided for the house staff who were to be responsible for following up the head's talk in assembly and the notice which was displayed throughout the school. The fact that house staff were to present these norms to the pupils emphasized the role of the houses in presenting the school's *behavioural norms*.

The practices themselves emphasized the physical and social structure of the school together with the importance of houses and house heads. House blocks other than their own were only to be entered on invitation from a pupil or a teacher in another house, and within these blocks the house head's office was only to be entered with permission from a teacher. The relative importance which the headmaster attached to the houses and to the heads of houses was therefore implicitly communicated to the pupils. The points of practice also emphasized the position of head of house and the power which these teachers had over the day-to-day lives and activities of the pupils. The pupils' appearance (in terms of cleanliness, tidiness, hair length and girls' make-up) was to be determined by individual house heads. The head of house was also responsible for seeing that pupils came to McGregor in school uniform. Only house heads could give pupils permission to leave the school site during the day, to bring sandwiches to school or to go home to lunch, and to bring a bicycle to school.

> R. G. Burgess, *Experiencing Comprehensive Education: A Study of Bishop McGregor School*, 1983, pp. 43–5.

Questions
1. *What do you understand by 'consensus' (para. 1)? Illustrate your answer by making reference to the headmaster's assembly talk.*
2. *How would you use the following concepts to analyse the headmaster's assembly talk? (i) power; (ii) control; (iii) authority.*
3. *What are 'behavioural norms' (para. 3)?*
4. *Discuss the way in which school rules can highlight aspects of school structure.*

RITUAL IN SCHOOL: CONSENSUS AND DIFFERENTIATION

School assemblies, uniforms and privileges are all part of school ritual. In this reading we turn to an analysis of ritual and ceremony in school organisation. As in many other areas of education, Bernstein has outlined a conceptual scheme that can be used by others to analyse school ritual. It is this conceptual scheme which is evaluated by Ronald King.

Reading 2

Ritual in Education

This paper has its origin in a lecture given to the Royal Society, and was first published, with Elvin and Peters as co-authors, in 1966. A slightly modified version appears in the Bernstein anthology (1975) without acknowledgement of the original co-authors.

Here the instrumental/expressive distinction is said to be associated with different forms of transmission and organization – the former *bureaucratic* and the latter by *rituals*. Examinations, testing and timetabling are all examples of the bureaucratic control of instrumental activities, but it should be pointed out that the expressive can be bureaucratized too, as with the use of school rules. Bernstein defines ritual as 'expression in action of ultimate values'. More practically I have suggested that in the school context, ritual consists of the use of *symbols*, where a symbol is either a pattern of behaviour or a *ceremonial*, or a physical *emblem*, representing something else. Bernstein's definition concerns what is supposedly symbolised. The rituals of the expressive order include the ceremonies of school assembly and the emblem of the school uniform. However, the instrumental order can be ritualized too, as in the award of points and prizes for school work and in the celebration of academic success at speech and prize days. The instrumental/expressive, bureaucratic/ritual dichotomies are therefore not in perfect fit.

Bernstein classifies school rituals into the 'consensual' and the 'differentiating'. *Consensual rituals*, including uniforms and school assemblies, 'function so as to bind together all members of the school, staff and pupils as a moral community, as a distinct collectivity'. This corresponds to what Waller (1932) called 'we feeling' – his book *The Sociology of Teaching* appears in the bibliography of the article. Durkheim's *The Elementary Forms of Religious Life* also appears in the bibliography and it is possible to see how Bernstein has taken Durkheim's analysis of rituals symbolizing the social order and applied it to the school. *'Differentiating' rituals* mark off groups within the school according to age, sex or 'social function', such as the prefectorial and house systems, and include the use of differences in uniform and the distribution of privileges. Bernstein does not mention another criterion of ritual differentiation – that of pupils' imputed ability. In over half of the seventy-two secondary schools I investigated the ceremonials of entry, position and exit of the school assembly were ability-stratified, with for example, the A stream behind the B, the B behind the C.

Bernstein's basic classification of rituals is not satisfactory in that all may have both consensual and differentiating 'functions'. If a 'consensual' ritual binds like-situated people together, a consequence must be to differentiate them from other people; similarly a 'successful' differentiating ritual would create internal consensus. This confusion seems to arise from Bernstein's assumptions of a general consensus among the participants as to the meaning of rituals, which relate to the reified schools' 'values'. Schools can't have values – only people. The empirical evidence that headteachers value the school assembly as symbolizing the school 'as a community', is clear (King, 1973). But this consensual purpose is not fulfilled, in that every one of thirty schools the majority of pupils expressed dislike of the school assembly; in fact, school assembly and uniform (another 'consensual' ritual) were the least liked aspects of school reported by pupils. Bernstein does suggest that pupils whose parents do not share, or do not understand, the expressive culture of the school 'may reject these "consensual" rituals, but there is no evidence to suggest any difference in pupils' self-reported rejection of assembly and uniform according to their fathers' occupations'.

Bernstein discusses the variability of ritual using the models of the 'stratified' and 'differentiated' schools. In 'stratified' schools pupils groups are arranged by age, sex and imputed ability, each considered to be a fixed attribute, and these differences between pupils are ritualized. In 'differentiated' schools these attributes are not considered to be fixed; consequently there is less use of ritual, and a greater use of 'personalized' or 'therapeutic' control, as relationships between teachers and pupils are those of 'co-operation' rather than the 'domination' of the 'stratified' school. In a section that anticipates his next paper, 'Open schools, open society?' Bernstein suggests that the increasing specialization of the work order which accompanies industrialization increases the importance of the instrumental order of the school and brings the move towards 'differentiated' social structures. This deritualization also arises from the posed lack of consensus in the 'central value system', echoing a point made in the 'Consensus' paper. Here we may see the influence of Durkheim's *The Division of Labour in Society* (which curiously is not in the bibliography), an influence acknowledged by Bernstein in later papers and discussed in their connection.

The 'Ritual' paper drew attention to an aspect of school organization ignored since Waller (1932); 'School ceremonies mostly have value, *or are thought to have value,* in the mobilization of individual attitudes with reference to group objectives' (my italics). However, Bernstein, by mainly taking the superordinate, headteacherly, view, assumes the purposes of ritual to be fulfilled (unlike Waller), that is, they are functionally consensual.

R. King, *The Sociology of School Organization*, 1983, pp. 40–2.

Questions

1. *What do you understand by the term 'ritual' (para. 2)?*
2. *On what basis would you distinguish between 'consensual rituals' and 'differentiating rituals' in a school (para. 3)?*
3. *Examine the rituals that occur in your school or college (i) weekly; (ii) termly; (iii) yearly. What is the purpose of these rituals?*

SCHOOL SUBCULTURES

In the course of conducting an ethnographic study of Lumley boys' Secondary Modern School David Hargreaves focused on the way in which differentiation took place. He analysed the relationship between school organisation and the peer group, and argued that two opposed subcultures existed among streams in the fourth year.

Reading 3

In the academic *subculture*, because the boys behave in conformity to teacher expectations, and because the two sets of values are consistent, the teacher is able to exert considerable control over the peer group. In the delinquescent subculture, the teachers have little power of social control, because of the conflict which exists between teacher and pupil values. Attempts to change the culture of low streams must thus begin with the conversion of the leaders or high status boys. When teachers regard the high status low stream boys as 'worthless louts' with whom they cannot afford to 'waste time', they are in fact discarding not only these few boys, but also their only means by which group change might be effected.

The members of the delinquescent subculture, if our contention that they are status-deprived is just, reject the system which
confers this status and the values on which the status-system is
based. Such boys are thus forced to seek a substitute system
which can confer prestige in proportion to the degree of rejection
of the school's values. It is through the anti-academic rejection of
the school's values that informal status within the delinquescent
group is achieved. They reject the pupil role and replace it with
an autonomous and independent peer culture. Conformity thus
becomes more important than in the academic subculture, where
the boys are united through *individual* effort in academic
competition. In the delinquescent subculture self-esteem is a
collective product, since it can be obtained only in relation to the
group as a whole, that is, through conformity to anti-academic
group pressures, whereas in the academic subculture boys can
develop self-esteem on the more individualistic basis of academic
competence.

The members of the delinquescent subculture, then, seek
alternatives to the pupil role as defined by the teachers. Their
rejection of the pupil role is supported by the evidence in earlier
chapters and need not be repeated here. The important point is
that in re-defining the pupil role, such boys aspire to roles outside
the terms of the school. Although the low stream pupil is legally
forced to come to school, his status as a schoolboy is resented.
One solution is to re-define the pupil role in terms of *adult* roles,
as well as behaving in ways opposed to teacher definitions. The
rejection of the pupil role and the associated status system leads
to admiration and premature imitation of adult roles beyond the
school. This aspiration towards adult roles is a measure of the
rejection of the pupil role, for these boys anticipate their adult
socialization before they take up the appropriate work-role
outside the school. This premature and anticipatory adult
socialization expresses itself in the exaggerated display of selected
aspects of behaviour associated with adult status. Members of the
delinquescent subculture thus exhibit behaviour which symbolizes
adult status, for example, smoking and drinking. The delinquent
group smoked more cigarettes per day than any other group at
Lumley and they frequently drank bottles of cheap wine or sherry
in secret. To consume nicotine and alcohol, and to be seen to
consume them, compensates for their lack of satisfaction in the
pupil role. One of the reasons why many members of the
delinquescent subculture were so anxious to leave school was

because they wanted to have their status at *home* changed from being a 'school boy' into a 'worker', for as workers they would be allowed to smoke openly at home and would no longer have to run errands for the family. As Derek replied when I asked him what would be the nicest thing about starting work:

Walking in the house at night with a fag in my gob.

We need no longer wonder why the billiard hall was such an attraction to low stream boys.

D. H. Hargreaves, *Social Relations in a Secondary School*, 1967, pp. 172–3.

Questions

1. *What do you understand by the term 'subculture' (para. 1)?*
2. *Compare and contrast the academic and delinquescent subcultures.*
3. *To what extent does the formal organisation of the school and the peer group influence pupil behaviour?*
4. *What questions would you pose in order to investigate whether David Hargreaves' findings apply in (i) a girls' secondary school (ii) a coeducational comprehensive school?*

DIFFERENTIATION AND POLARISATION

While David Hargreaves worked in Lumley Secondary Modern School, Colin Lacey was examining the social mechanisms of schooling in a boys' grammar school. Lacey looked at the effects of secondary school selection and established a model of the process of subculture formation within the student body.

Reading 4

Differentiation. There are a number of scales on which a master habitually rates a boy. For the purpose of the analysis, two will be considered:

(a) *Academic Scale.*
(b) *Behaviour Scale.* This would include considerations as varied as general classroom behaviour and attitudes; politeness; attention; helpfulness; time spent in school societies and sports.

The two are not independent. Behaviour affects academic standards not only because good behaviour involves listening and attending but because a master becomes favourably disposed towards a boy who is well behaved and trying hard. The teacher therefore tends to help him and even to mark him up. I have found in my own marking of books that when I know the form (i.e. the good and bad pupils), I mark much more quickly. For example, I might partly read an essay and recognise the writing: 'Oh, Brown. Let's see, he tries hard. Good, neat work, missed one or two ideas – seven out of ten.' Or 'This is a bit scruffy – no margin, not underlined; seems to have got the hang of it though. Who is it? Oh, Jones, that nuisance – five out of ten!'

Polarisation. There is another reason why good behaviour is correlated with academic achievement. A boy who does well and wishes to do well academically is predisposed to accept the grammar school's system of values, that is, he behaves well. The system gives him high prestige, and it is therefore in his interest to support it; the correlation between membership of the choir and performance in class illustrates this point. He is supporting his position of prestige. On the other hand, a boy who does badly academically is predisposed to criticise, reject or even sabotage the system where he can, since it places him in an inferior position.

A boy showing the extreme development of this phenomenon may subscribe to values which are actually the inverted values of the school. He obtains prestige for cheeking a teacher, playing truant, not doing homework, for smoking, drinking and even stealing. As it develops, the anti-group produces its own impetus. The boy who takes refuge in such a group because his work is poor finds that the group commits him to a behaviour pattern which means that his work will stay poor – and in fact often gets progressively worse.

The following extracts from an essay entitled 'Abuse', written by a first-form boy for his housemaster, illustrate a development of anti-group values which is extreme for a first-year pupil:

> I am writing this essay about abuse in the toilets . . . What they [the prefects] call abuse and what I call abuse are two different things altogether.
>
> All the people where I live say I am growing up to be a 'Ted' so I try to please them by acting as much like one as I possibly can. I go around kicking a ball against the wall that is nearest to their house and making as much noise as I can and I intend to carry on doing this until they can leave me

alone . . . It seems to me the Grammar School knows nothing about abuse for *I would much rather be a hooligan and get some fun out of life than be a snob always being the dear little nice boy doing what he is told* [my italics].

C. Lacey, *Hightown Grammar: The School as a Social System*, 1970, pp. 57–8.

Questions
1. *On the basis of Lacey's discussion, how would you distinguish between differentiation and polarisation?*
2. *Outline and discuss the relationship that Lacey identifies between good behaviour and academic achievement.*
3. *In what ways does the essay on 'Abuse' illustrate a development of anti-group values?*

MIXED ABILITY GROUPING IN THE COMPREHENSIVE SCHOOL

With the development of comprehensive schools different patterns of school organisation could be compared. David Newbold's study examined the social and academic consequences of streaming and mixed ability grouping using standardised and school-based tests and survey results. He concludes that mixed ability organisation results in social advantages without academic disadvantages.

Reading 5

If the comprehensive school has succeeded in integrating pupils of all abilities and backgrounds into one community, then this should show itself in the way in which they choose their friends, at school or elsewhere. At the age of 12 or 13 the choice of friends in the away-from-school context is likely to be limited by geographical considerations, but within school there is no such local constraint. An indication that pupils choose to spend their time at school, but out of the classroom, with friends from different ability groups or social backgrounds will suggest that the integrating function of the school is succeeding. It may be that this is looking at social integration on a very limited front, but more powerful or longer-term indicators are not yet available for this age range. It would be unrealistic to expect that there would be no tendency, whatever the organizational system, for pupils to choose to associate with others of similar interests or characteristics, of which ability and background are a part. The question is whether in one system of ability grouping in a school, the tendency towards intellectual and social integration is greater than in the other.

The findings at Banbury suggest clearly that the form unit, which is both the pastoral and working unit, provides the base for friendships to develop, and that this gradually outweighs the long-standing influence of former primary school associations, unless these two factors have been linked. Where the primary school has been the basis of allocation to forms it is not surprising to find that its influence remains powerful, but if the children are dispersed between forms at 11+ then the strength of the primary school bond is dissipated. There is evidence that children tend to associate with others of their own ability, but this is significantly and markedly less in the mixed ability forms than in the streamed forms. Not only is there more opportunity for children of differing abilities to meet more easily when they are based on mixed ability forms, it actually happens that they take advantage of it at all ability levels. Whether or not these friendships last, or the children discriminate more in terms of ability and background as they grow older, is not yet known. Nevertheless, the analyses have shown clearly that in the lower secondary age range there is a greater degree of mixing between ability groups in the mixed ability than in the streamed system.

Friendship analyses by social background are not so amenable to definitive analysis as those by ability grouping. Social classes are less capable of consistent and reliable classification since the allocation to a socioeconomic group of any particular job or profession is somewhat arbitrary, and is likely to vary with the promotion structure of particular employers and with changing economic circumstances over a period of time. The socio-economic classification of the working population as published by the Registrar General has been used in the analyses at Banbury, but in this the Group 3 (middle) class is dominant. This has meant that inter-class friendship choices are necessarily limited in quantity, and so the fact that significant conclusions have emerged from the analyses in this study is the more important – even though at first sight they may appear statistically less powerful than, say, for the ability analyses already discussed.

In the analyses of friendship associations by socioeconomic class, the evidence from this study is for greater mixing in the mixed ability system, and it is particularly important to find that the two Halls in the mixed ability system and the two Halls in the streamed system, all considered individually, support this conclusion. This result is confirmed too by analyses of first choice friends only, and also of boys and girls separately. As when verbal reasoning ability is used as the friendship-association criterion, there is an underlying tendency in both grouping systems for pupils to choose from their own social class: this is likely to be associated with home, geographical, and primary school of origin factors. However, the evidence is there that greater mixing between social classes does occur in friendship choice amongst the younger secondary pupils in the mixed ability system.

D. Newbold, *Ability Grouping – the Banbury Enquiry*, 1977, pp. 110–11.

Questions

1. *What evidence does Newbold provide on the relationship between friendship choice and school organisation?*
2. *Assess Newbold's evidence on the relationship between social class and friendship choice in the mixed ability system.*
3. *Outline and discuss the methods you would use to replicate Newbold's study in the upper secondary age range of a school.*
4. *Newbold states 'If the comprehensive school has succeeded in integrating pupils of all abilities and backgrounds into one community, then this should show itself in the way they choose their friends, at school or elsewhere' (para. 1). Do you agree?*

MIXED ABILITY TEACHING AND COMPREHENSIVE IDEOLOGIES

Stephen Ball's study of Beachside Comprehensive School follows in the tradition of Hargreaves and Lacey. He examined social processes associated with school organization by focusing on banding and mixed ability groups. His analysis of mixed ability teaching demonstrates a gap between the rhetoric and the reality of comprehensive schooling.

Reading 6

In terms of the grouping of pupils and the organization of the curriculum, at least in some subjects, the introduction of mixed-ability obviously represents the sort of change in the internal structure of the school advocated by egalitarian comprehensivists. It also provides greatly increased possibilities for the achievement of the aims of social mixing and social tolerance advocated by the social-engineering supporters of comprehensive education, and the aims of greater equality of opportunity advocated by the meritocratic supporters. However, as we have seen, little of the innovation debate at Beachside was couched in these terms. And, as noted . . . the 'organizing notions' in the teachers' working assumptions about the mixed-ability classroom tend to perpetuate a view of the classroom predicated upon the 'typing' and differentiation of pupils according to the single criterion of achieved-ability. Furthermore, when the physical separation of pupils does take place, through setting and then through the formation of O-level and C.S.E. classes in the fourth and fifth years, in the case-study form at least, the middle-class pupils are over-represented in top sets and O-level courses. In addition, the mixed-ability grouping creates, in effect a situation where many fewer working-class pupils have the opportunity to experience major success roles in the classroom, because of the tendency of middle-class children to dominate the top positions in examinations and tests. This may also go a long way to account for the almost exact 'fit' between option choices and option allocations in the case-study form at the end of the third year . . . In the context of banding it was possible for pupils in bands 2 and 3 to be top of the form and still be regarded by their teachers as 'not up to much adacemically', thus creating a mismatch between warming-up and cooling-out experiences, and producing in some cases what were regarded as 'inappropriate' option choices – that is, over-aspiration. This did not occur in the mixed-ability forms. Thus, it would seem that so long as schooling continues to be seen by teachers as a stage of preparation for what succeeds it, and achieved ability is the single, and narrowly-defined, criterion for success in school, then the pupils' experience of education will inevitably be one of competition within a rigid hierarchy of rewards and esteem.

Schools are not autonomous and neutral institutions, and education is not simply a universal good, as much of the rhetoric surrounding comprehensive education and mixed-ability grouping appears to assume. The evidence of this study of the practice of comprehensive schooling suggests that, rather than being a profound egalitarian change in our education system, as is often suggested by 'utopian romantic idealists' in educational literature, mixed-ability grouping in fact represents a new ideology of implementation in the British school, which replaces more traditional ideologies whose legitimacy has been called into question. At the ideological level, the *Black Paper* writers present mixed-ability grouping as a fundamental challenge to existing educational practices and values, and yet this study suggests that such challenges are by no means a necessary part of introducing mixed-ability groups. Indeed, continuity of traditional practices may be all too easily achieved. If this is true of comprehensive schools generally, then, in Turner's terms, even the comprehensive school which introduces mixed-ability is 'securing a system of sponsorship mobility behind a context mask' (Woods 1976: 146). From this perspective the 'comprehensive debate', the publicly-rehearsed advocacy of and opposition to comprehensive education, may be seen to be totally divorced from the realities of comprehensive schooling. If Beachside is at all typical, then in terms of teachers' practices, comprehensive schools do not represent a socialist alternative to the 'selective' system. Indeed, when viewed in relation to current practice in the comprehensive school the 'comprehensive debate' appears merely to be a form of ideological in-fighting between the conservative, the rationalizing and the democratic schools of thought in British education.

S. J. Ball, *Beachside Comprehensive: A Case Study of Secondary Schooling*, 1981, pp. 288–90.

Questions

1. *What would appear to be the advantages of mixed ability grouping in the comprehensive school?*
2. *How did mixed ability grouping actually work in Beachside Comprehensive?*
3. *To what extent do you share Stephen Ball's views on school organisation and comprehensive education? Give reasons for your answer.*

SECONDARY SCHOOLS AND THEIR EFFECTS ON CHILDREN

One of the most widely quoted pieces of research conducted in the late 1970s was a study by Michael Rutter and his colleagues of twelve Inner London secondary schools which attempted to address the question: what effects do schools have on children? In the following extract they discuss their conclusions on school processes.

Reading 7

School process: a causal influence?

We have suggested that there is a causal relationship between school process and children's progress. Firm conclusions about causation can only come from controlled experimental studies. The only way to be sure that school practices actually influence children's behaviour and attainments is to alter those practices and then determine if this results in changes in the children's progress. In a non-experimental study, the *pattern* of statistical associations can nevertheless provide quite good guidance as to whether a relationship is likely to reflect a casual effect.

In the present study, the existence of longitudinal data was particularly helpful in showing that the pupil outcomes were associated with experiences which occurred during the years of secondary schooling. Not only did the schools differ in outcome after controlling for the children's measured characteristics at intake, but also these differences in outcome were systematically associated with measured features of the schools.

But perhaps the most crucial point concerns the pattern of correlations with school process. The question here is whether schools were as they were because of the children they admitted, or rather whether children behaved in the way they did because of school influences. Of course, interactions will take place in both directions, but the much greater correlation between school process and children's behaviour/attainments at the *end* of secondary schooling strongly implies a greater effect of schools on children than of children on schools. We may infer that it is very likely that school processes *do* influence pupil outcome.

Of course it was not suggested that the links work only in one direction. As we have already discussed, schools constitute just one element in a complex set of ecological interactions, and are shaped and constrained by a variety of societal forces outside their immediate control. They are likely to be influenced by the types of neighbourhood they serve; running a school in a remote country village is not the same as running one in inner London. Factors such as the extent of parental support and community involvement are also liable to influence how a school functions as a social unit. The teaching task in an academically selective school serving a prosperous middle-class district will be very different from that in a school with a heavy preponderance of less able pupils from socially disadvantaged homes.

Our study was not able to look at variations of this kind, but they are clearly important issues. Even within a similar geographical area, external influences, and perhaps most importantly the pupils themselves, will play a part in shaping school life. The initial teaching task is shaped by the attitudes, behaviour, interests and capabilities of the children in the class. Teacher actions then influence children's behaviour, which in turn modifies teacher behaviour, which then further impinges on the children. In this way, spirals of either improving or deteriorating behaviour (and attainments) seem likely to be built up.

The pattern of connections is complex. It is nevertheless clear that within this network, schools have a considerable degree of choice in how they are organised, and that teachers have a similar choice in their decisions on how to respond to the children they teach. Our results suggest that these decisions on how to respond are likely to affect the chances of the children improving in their behaviour and attainments.

It is not argued that schools are the *most* important influence on children's progress, and we agree with Bernstein that education cannot compensate for the inequities of society. Nevertheless, we do suggest that schools constitute one major area of influence, and one which is susceptible to change.

M. Rutter, B. Maughan, P. Mortimore and J. Ouston, *Fifteen Thousand Hours: Secondary Schools and Their Effects on Children*, 1979, pp. 180–2.

Questions
1. *What do you understand by (i) an experimental study (ii) a non-experimental study in education?*
2. *What are the main conclusions drawn about school processes?*
3. *Compare and contrast the* social *factors that will influence the operation of a remote village school and a school in a large city.*

A CRITIQUE OF THE RUTTER RESEARCH
Research is often surrounded by interest, discussion, debate and

on occasion some controversy. The work of Rutter and his colleagues in *Fifteen Thousand Hours* was no exception as it aroused interest and controversy over its methods of study, its findings and areas which reviewers argued the team had overlooked. In this reading, David Reynolds discusses the conclusions on school process.

Reading 8

In general, although the authors' suggestion that individual schools' academic and social performance is partially independent from outside structural influences seems to be supported by their empirical evidence and analysis, there must remain substantial doubts as to exactly how large the school's contribution to that performance is. Rutter *et al.* principally use individual pupils' verbal reasoning score and occupational group in their attempt to control for the effect of intake variation upon outcome, yet there are many other factors – such as type of housing tenure or level of parental income – which previous research suggests as important influences upon school outcomes. It must be regarded as a major flaw that the authors nowhere discuss the possibility that the *variables* that have been used may only make a partial adjustment for the effect of intake differences. Furthermore, the adjustments performed for balance of intake (after the earlier adjustment for actual intake scores) used only three categories of verbal reasoning score, although seven categories were reported earlier in the book. It may well be that – since one-half of the pupils fall into the middle category – the lack of sensitivity of this measure may again be responsible for a substantial underestimate of intake and balance effects upon output.

One's major criticisms of the book, however, must be reserved for the authors' discussions of 'school process' and of the way in which such processes are held to affect school success. Chapter ten attempts to link together findings about the relationship of individual school process items – such as pupil use of school library or rate of corporal punishment – with findings on school outcome and discusses the various aspects of the school regimes by means of grouping together the process factors under such classifications as 'Group management in the classroom', 'School values and norms of behaviour', or 'Contra school peer groups'. The literature on which this discussion is based, however, is drawn heavily from the psychological literature (as in the discussion of group norms, models and teacher expectations) or from the literature on the sociology or social psychology of organisations (as in the discussion on general conditions and staff attitudes to pupils), and consequently neglects almost completely the important ethnographic and micro-sociological literature on within-school processes that has accumulated since the paradigmatic revolution caused by the new sociology of education. Where sociological literature is mentioned, discussion is brief, generally banal and grossly over-simplified, as the discussion on page 199 of 'Contra school peer groups' indicates when it suggests that:

> In Britain, Sugarman (1967) suggested that youth culture was linked with a thoroughgoing alienation from school; Webb (1962) saw the issue as a contest over control; and Delamont (1976) has described the various strategies followed by teacher and pupil protagonists. Other writers have seen the struggle more as an extension of the social conflicts inherent in Western societies (see review by Karabel & Halsey, 1977). Undoubtedly there is a good deal [*sic*] in these views of schooling, although sometimes the evidence has been stretched rather thin in reaching dramatic conclusions (see Davies, 1976, for a critique of some of the views on social control and education).

Certainly there is a place in any book of this kind for the 'normal science' of a literature review that places a research report in its disciplinary context. However, this sometimes undigested and often indigestible review – surprisingly written by Rutter himself – is simply inadequate for that task.

In short, the book lacks *a sociological imagination* and fails to link together the structural factors of the schools that the authors have studied with the consciousness of the pupils that is reflected in the pupils' differing levels of rebellion, truancy and achievement. The authors do not adequately describe, then, *how* the factors have their effects and *how* the factors relate to each other to form a 'school ethos' or 'school process'. The authors also do not discuss *why* it is that the schools exist in the form that they do. Are differences in teacher strategies and methods a reflection of ideological differences between groups of staff as to how they perceive the aims of education? Are they merely pragmatic, situational adaptations? Do they reflect variations in teacher ability, character or background? Do these current differences in school methods and/or personnel actually *reflect* past differences between the schools in their overall success? How have the schools come to be what they are? Certainly these issues are difficult ones to explore – given the paucity of work at a school level from which to draw leads – but they deserved much greater attention than they received in this study.

In many respects, then, the book reflects upon an opportunity that has been missed. Although it seems likely that schools do have an independent effect, the size of that effect and the explanation for its nature are still unclear.

D. Reynolds, 'Review symposium: *Fifteen Thousand Hours*', *British Journal of Sociology of Education*, 1980, pp. 209–10.

Questions
1. *On what basis does Reynolds claim that there must be doubts on the effect schools have on pupil performance?*
2. (i) *What are Reynolds's major criticisms of the Rutter teams' view of 'school process'?*
   (ii) *Do you agree with Reynolds? Give reasons for your answer.*
3. *What are 'variables' (para. 1) in social research? What 'variables' can be used in research on education, schools and schooling?*
4. *Reynolds claims that* Fifteen Thousand Hours *lacks 'a sociological imagination' (para. 4). What does this appear to mean in relation to this study?*

ESSAY QUESTIONS
1. Select a published study of a school and evaluate its contribution to sociological understanding. (AEB, 1982)
2. Evaluate sociological contributions to our understanding of *either* public schools *or* comprehensive schools *or* primary schools.
3. Do patterns of school organisation affect educational achievement?
4. Discuss the ways in which school rules are transmitted and applied.

FURTHER READING
There is now a vast literature that examines the social processes involved in school organisation. The following list is subdivided into commentaries on the school and studies of schools.

Commentaries on the School
1. R. King, *The Sociology of School Organization*, Methuen, 1983.
   Provides a basic introduction to the main theoretical perspectives in

this area of study together with illustrations from British empirical studies.

2. J. Mortimore and T. Blackstone, *Disadvantage and Education*, Heinemann, 1982.

Contains a review of the literature on school factors involved in educational disadvantage.

Studies of Schools

1. S. J. Ball, *Beachside Comprehensive: A Case Study of Secondary Schooling*, Cambridge University Press, 1981.

Provides a discussion of banding and mixed ability grouping in a comprehensive school.

2. R. G. Burgess, *Experiencing Comprehensive Education: A Study of Bishop McGregor School*, Methuen, 1983.

Provides an analysis of the way in which a comprehensive school works. There are chapters on the headmaster's conception of the school, the house and departmental system, and the organisation of non-academic work.

3. D. H. Hargreaves, *Social Relations in a Secondary School*, Routledge and Kegan Paul, 1967.

A case study of a secondary modern school that focuses on the school subculture.

4. R. King, *All Things Bright and Beautiful? A Sociological Study of Infants' Classrooms*, Wiley, 1978.

Provides an interesting account of infant school classes.

5. C. Lacey, *Hightown Grammar: the School as a Social System*, Manchester University Press, 1970.

Provides a detailed study of a boys' grammar school and focuses on differentiation.

6. M. Rutter, B. Maughan, P. Mortimore and J. Ouston, *Fifteen Thousand Hours: Secondary Schools and their Effects on Children*, Open Books, 1979.

Examines the characteristics of children *and* organisational variables in twelve Inner London schools.

7. R. Sharp and A. Green, *Education and Social Control*, Routledge and Kegan Paul, 1975.

An observational study of a progressive primary school.

8. J. Wakeford, *The Cloistered Elite*, Macmillan, 1969.

Provides a sociological account of life in an English boarding school.

9. W. Waller, *The Sociology of Teaching*, Wiley, 1967 (originally published in 1932).

The classic study of teaching that provides sociological insights into patterns of everyday life that occur in schools.

6

The social processes of classroom life

Although sociologists of education have focused their attention upon schools, it is only in the last ten years that they have begun to examine what happens in the classroom, what social processes occur, what are the main patterns of social interaction and what are their implications for teaching and learning.

A range of theoretical approaches have been used to study classrooms, although in Britain, symbolic interactionism has been most popular. Nevertheless, attempts have been made by classroom researchers to combine interactionism with phenomenology and to use interactionism, phenomenology and Marxism alongside one another. Many researchers who use these approaches pose questions about the process of classroom interaction and the perspectives that are adopted by teachers and pupils. Accordingly, classroom researchers use ethnographic methods of investigation that include observation, participant observation, informal or unstructured interviews and documentary materials. However, these methods cannot be used in a uniform way and therefore several researchers who have worked in this tradition and whose work is included in this chapter have published accounts of how they went about conducting classroom research.

Much research has taken place in secondary school classrooms, especially in the state sector. Here, researchers have concentrated on particular phases of social life in classrooms such as the initial encounters that occur between teachers and pupils and perspectives and strategies that have been used by teachers and pupils in the course of interaction. Many of these research areas are very familiar and therefore difficult to study. However, the familiarity of classrooms can be analysed using sociological concepts. For example, Sara Delamont (1981) has suggested how the familiarity of the classroom and classroom routine can be questioned by scrutinising sex roles. The result is that by using the concept of 'gender' the sociologist not only learns more about the use of sex roles in the classroom but also about other classroom processes that are thrown into sharp relief.

The readings in this chapter have been grouped around three themes. The first is initial encounters in the classroom (Ball; Edwards and Furlong; Hargreaves, Hester and Mellor). While each of these passages follows the same theme, they adopt a different perspective. Stephen Ball's study is interactionist, while Edwards and Furlong focus on language in classroom interaction and Hargreaves, Hester and Mellor utilise an interactionist/ phenomenological approach to construct a theory about how teachers get to know their pupils and typify their actions. Each of these approaches helps the researcher to focus on different things that occur during initial classroom encounters. In short, these different approaches complement each other rather than provide an account of 'what is really happening'.

A second group of readings by Woods, Delamont and Burgess highlight different strategies that are used by teachers and pupils in classrooms. Peter Woods has outlined eight strategies that teachers can use to survive in the classroom: domination, negotiation, socialisation, fraternisation, absence or removal, ritual and routine, occupational therapy and morale-boosting. It is these strategies that are used to handle incidents and involve 'the avoidance of incident, the masking or disguising of incident, the weathering of incident and the neutralizing of incident' (Woods, 1979, p. 146). Meanwhile, pupils also adopt strategies so that they can survive in the classroom. Sara Delamont indicates how bargaining can occur between the teacher and pupils during the course of marking test papers, while Robert Burgess highlights how teachers and pupils redefine situations during lessons. Here, the key issue involves a consideration of the range of strategies that can be used by teachers and pupils in the classroom.

The last two readings in this chapter focus on the way in which the concept 'gender' highlights some classroom processes. Michelle Stanworth's research in a further education college demonstrates the different ways in which boys and girls are treated in the classroom and the ways in which identities are structured through basic classroom processes. Meanwhile, Mary Fuller takes up the issue of race and gender through an analysis of the classroom behaviour of West Indian girls. Here, she indicates the complexity involved in classroom life and how sociologists cannot just look for an answer in their quest to understand classroom interaction.

In the course of examining school classrooms, sociologists working within an interactionist perspective have considered such questions as: what happens in classroom encounters between teachers and pupils? How do teachers and pupils interpret classroom life? How are classroom processes defined and redefined? What strategies are adopted in the classroom? How are identities structured in the classroom?

Classrooms are familiar social settings where sociologists can begin to explore the social processes involved in schooling. Here, different theoretical perspectives complement each other and help to extend our knowledge of classroom activities. However, there are still many problems to resolve not least of which is the relationship between microscopic analyses of the processes that occur in classrooms and macroscopic accounts of the operation of educational systems.

INITIAL ENCOUNTERS IN THE CLASSROOM

By focusing on the pattern of interaction involved in a first classroom encounter, Stephen Ball is able to highlight the developmental nature of teacher–pupil relationships. He examines the ways in which strategies are tested out and rules established. His material complements the analyses provided by Tony Edwards and John Furlong and by David Hargreaves and his associates.

Reading 1

It was clear both from my observation and interview data that these initial encounters were recognised both by teachers and pupils as a distinct phase in the history of their interaction. For example:

> It's depressing to know that whenever you have a new class that for the first few lessons you're going to have fun and games until you show them who's boss. (Maths teacher)

> They're scared they don't know who you are, then they find out you're not a Harry Jones [teacher renowned for being very strict with pupils] or you haven't got the charisma of David Lortimer [teacher renowned for having excellent relations with pupils]. (English teacher)

> **SB** What happens usually when you have a new teacher?
> **Band 2 pupil** We're nice to him the first day then real horrible, you have to get used to him first.
> **Band 2 pupil** The boys muck about to see if they can get away with being stupid.

From the pupils' point of view these initial encounters necessitate a *testing out* of the new teacher. This normally involves two *stages*, the first is a passive and in a sense, purely observational stage. This is indicated by the first pupil quoted above, 'we're nice to him the first day', and was noted by all the student teachers I interviewed. For example:

> In the first lesson they were very quiet. (English student)

> They're quiet at first because they don't know where they stand. (Geography student)

As a general statement the rowdiest forms are quiet in the first lesson. (Physics student)

This stage in the development of their relationships with pupils was referred to by some teachers and students as 'the honeymoon': it rarely appeared to last beyond the first lesson. Hargreaves refers to this as the 'Disciplinary Illusion'. After this the second stage is embarked upon, which usually involves at least some pupils in being 'real horrible'. This is when the pupils are actually involved in what Wadd refers to as 'elementary escalation', playing up the teacher.

. . . to see if the teacher is prepared to defend the authority he is seeking to establish.

This stage of testing out through playing up the teacher is evident in the following observation notes collected in an early lesson of a new school year involving a religious studies teacher and a third year, band two class. The class arrives in groups of four or five over a two or three minute period. The teacher is already in the classroom and is standing at the front of the room with her arms crossed. She is pointedly 'waiting' for the class to arrive and to pay attention. Teacher:

You're taking a long time to settle down. (This descriptive comment is clearly intended to reduce the volume of the noise being made by the pupils, and to indicate that the teacher wants their attention. This is the function of the teacher's talk here.)

Two boys, Keith and Charlie, are being particularly noisy and there is considerable confusion, Keith and Charlie are talking out loud and making comments across the room ignoring the teacher. The teacher shouts at the class to be quiet and then immediately sends Charlie out. The class is then threatened with 35 minutes detention and the amount of noise decreases considerably. Keith is now reading as instructed, but he seems intent on annoying the teacher. He turns round in his chair again and waves out of the window. The teacher again addresses the class as a whole.

I'm very annoyed with you and I shall show you how annoyed I am by punishing you.

Keith begins to do some work but is still making noises in his throat. He is going as far as he can, pushing the teacher to the limits of her tolerance, the teacher's response is to delineate the steps towards that limit.

> That's your last warning Keith, any more and you shall be in detention.

He tests and pushes and she lays down the rules. What is expected, what is allowed, what is not, Keith is moved to the front, he is now quiet. The teacher calls for silence.

> I'm not satisfied with the standard of work, anyone who talks will be in detention for an hour tomorrow night.

The teacher asserts herself gradually and imposes her definition of the way the classroom should be, over the attempts to assert an alternative definition by some of the class. Her expectations of work and behaviour are made very clear. But the class were alert to the way in which she would treat Keith and Charlie, their behaviour tending to respond to the way in which these two were handled. When Keith is finally subdued the teacher is able to impose an unbroken rule of silence on the whole class.

> S. J. Ball, 'Initial encounters in the classroom and the process of establishment', in P. Woods (ed), *Pupil Strategies: Explorations in the Sociology of the School*, 1980, pp. 146–8.

Questions
1. *What 'stages' (para. 2) are involved in initial classroom encounters between teachers and pupils?*
2. *What constitutes 'testing out' (para. 2) in the classroom?*
3. *How would you analyse the teacher's interaction with her pupils?*

SETTLING INTO THE CLASSROOM

Tony Edwards and John Furlong focus on classroom talk in first year pupils' humanities lessons at the Abraham Moss Centre in Manchester. They consider: what needs to be said? How much needs to be said? How do pupils and teachers sustain their classroom identities? Talk is used to examine how teachers and pupils handled initial classroom encounters.

Reading 2

First lessons are always difficult. In Abraham Moss, some normal difficulties were intensified. The children came from a large number of primary schools, so that they were usually strangers to one another. The unfamiliar label for this part of their timetable meant that past experience of history or geography was not obviously of much use, and there were no ready-made frames of reference such as the traditional school subjects provide. In the particular lessons we observed, sixty pupils were gathered together in an open area too confined to allow much scope for confusion. In these conditions, organizational matters took precedence. The children had to learn to come in quickly, find their places, get the materials necessary for work, and appear busy. All these activities can be summarized as '*getting down to work*'.

Classrooms are about work. They are places of purposeful activity, even when the purposes of the actual activity taking place are not at all clear. That pupils should appear to be busy most of the time is a general rule that only needs to be recalled and reinforced, rather than constructed anew with each group of pupils. Of course, knowledge of the *particular* forms of work required, of what it means to be appropriately busy in that part of the curriculum, is not something that can be taken for granted. But in these first lessons, what was done was less important than that *something* should be done. With so many children likely to be bothered and bewildered, the teachers had to free themselves to deal with the problems of individuals. The best way to do this was to give the less bewildered something to keep them occupied which looked like school-work. We 'knew' this from our own teaching experience, and our 'knowledge' was confirmed in conversation with the teachers themselves. Other reasons were made obvious in what was actually said at the time. For example, *at least* two things were being done in the following sequences (the 'at least' reminds us that beneath the surface of the interaction, the basic authority of the teacher was being announced and reinforced). Particular procedures were being established which would persist throughout the year, and an emphasis on self-directed learning was already being introduced. That this *was* what was happening in these early lessons was made explicit at several points:

5.2 T: OK, we'll do that, then. In future, when you come into this lesson, you come in, you put your bag on the floor by your place and then quickly go and get a booklet yourself, and you'll find that it works. You might think

that there'll be sixty kids all charging over there at the
same time, but it doesn't happen. You'll find that you'll
be able to come in, walk quietly over to the trolley, get
the booklet that you need, go back to your place, and
you'll be ready to start work : : : : Are *you* listening?

P: ((Nods.))

T: What are we going to do with your books?

P: Sir, you'll put them down on the trolley.

T: Right. You'll find your books on that trolley. ((Further
elaboration and repetition of the instructions.)) And
we'll see if that works. You'll be able to come in, get
your book, go and collect your booklet, sit down and
get down to work. In that way, we don't have to spend
ten minutes while you have to wait for everything to be
done – while you have to wait for us to start you off.
You'll be able to get yourself going all on your own.

In the following lesson, when many of the children were late
arriving in the open area, one of the teachers commented to the
other as they awaited the stragglers, 'I wonder if we'll need to say
anything, or if they'll be able to just come in and do it.' There
were compliments from both of them for one boy who was
'working away there – smashing. You can hear his brain ticking.
Straight into it.' There were also reproofs for those who 'should
be sitting down and working by now, like this lad, look, he's
away.' But it appeared that too many were still unable to 'just
come in and do it'.

5.3 T: Well, I'd like to compliment some people who came in
and worked very well. Some people came in straight-
away, they remembered what they had to do. They saw
the books and they saw the tray of booklets and they
came in and got on with it and sorted themselves
out : : : : If you come in and see the books out like
that, and if Mr — doesn't give you any instructions,
what should you do? : : : : What's the routine when
you come in, what should you do?

P: Sir, you get your books and start work. ((Starting work
is then elaborated again by one of the teachers.))

A. D. Edwards and V. J. Furlong, *The Language of Teaching*, 1978,
pp. 83–5.

Questions

1. *What is involved in 'getting down to work' (para. 1)?*
2. *What are the teachers transmitting to the pupils through classroom talk?*
3. *Discuss the ways in which teachers and pupils establish their classroom identities.*

GETTING TO KNOW PUPILS

How do teachers get to know new pupils? David Hargreaves and his colleagues suggest a theory of typing by which teachers get to know pupils. They suggest that teachers speculate about their pupils, elaborate their views on them and finally stabilise their opinions using a variety of materials.

Reading 3

When pupils arrive at their secondary school, they do not normally know their teachers and the teachers do not know them. It is tempting to think that as far as their new teachers are concerned, these eleven-year-old pupils are simply 'blanks', bare canvases that can only be filled in by the passage of time, or perhaps hidden pictures whose detail will be revealed by the passage of time. Yet this is not, in fact, the case. Certainly it is true that the teacher does not know them as individuals; at the first meeting they are pupils without names. But each teacher does know quite a lot about them in general or as a collectivity. They all have a history for the teacher, but it is a typical history, not an individual one.

In the first place, he knows that they are first year pupils. They have a common age-range; they come from a local area; they have recently left a primary school. If he has some experience as a secondary school teacher, he will have encountered first year pupils before. He knows what first year pupils have been like in the past, so he knows something about what to expect from this particular intake. Indeed he will probably use his past experience as a standard against which to judge these newcomers, and will soon be saying:

'They're the worst first year form I've ever had.'
'They're not settling down very quickly this year.'
'They're much more docile than the lot I had last year.'

He knows something about the school's catchment area. He knows that some pupils come from the 'better' districts, residential areas for professional people, and that others come from areas noted for 'problem' families. He knows something about the primary schools that 'feed' his school: that one school gives its pupils a 'traditional' education, whilst another is perhaps experimenting with highly 'progressive' methods. All this he knows from his *typifications* of schools and neighbourhoods, even though as yet he cannot attach particular pieces of information to any individual pupil.

If the teacher has record cards from the primary schools at his disposal, he may read them and discover the proportions of pupils coming from particular schools or areas – though in fact he is unlikely to do this unless he is the 'form-teacher'. (He may even have met the pupils on a visit to the primary school.) He may see a surname that he knows, and so realize or guess that this may be a brother or a sister of a pupil he has taught in the past. He may have some accidental information about a pupil. For instance, he may live in the same street as the pupil, or he may be a personal friend of one of the primary school teachers who has passed on some information.

So on the first day of term, when the teacher meets his pupils for the first time, he knows little about the vast majority of them. Over the next few weeks, he will 'get to know' them. He will learn to put names to faces and each pupil will emerge as a unique individual with his own personality and characteristics. Yet this formulation of pupils as persons is not a creation ex nihilo. Rather, each pupil is matched against some other material. First, he is matched against any pre-information that is passed to him by other teachers. Second he is matched against the teacher's conception of the typical first year pupil, which is an anonymous abstraction derived from all his previous experience of first year pupils. Third, he is matched against his peers – all the other first year pupils. The first two or three pupils to emerge as individuals serve as a kind of yardstick against which an emergent individual can be matched; a pupil is described as being 'similar to' or 'the opposite of' or 'not at all like' those pupils who have already acquired a degree of individuality. In the teachers' terms, within the first few days one or two pupils begin to 'stand out' from the rest, who remain temporarily 'unknown quantities' precisely because they do not stand out.

To discover what it is that leads a pupil to 'stand out' is to

discover some of the important forms or terms in which a pupil is
typed by teachers. Their early descriptions, or more accurately
their 'first impressions' of pupils, reveal the constructs they use to
formulate pupils. We approached this problem in two ways. We
asked teachers after two weeks of term which pupils had made
any impact on them; and we also provided teachers with a list of
pupils and asked them to comment on each name. Teachers, of
course, varied in the speed with which they 'got to know' the
pupils. Doubtless some teachers made a more active effort to do
this than others. But more important, some teachers had special
responsibility for certain groups of pupils, as tutors or form-
teachers, and so made special efforts in this direction. Further,
some teachers taught the pupils more often than others, and so
naturally made more rapid progress.

> D. H. Hargreaves, S. K. Hester and F. J. Mellor, *Deviance in
> Classrooms*, 1975, pp. 146–7.

Questions

1. *What do you understand by the term 'typification' (para. 2)? What
   resources can teachers use to typify pupils?*
2. *What stages are involved in the typification of pupils?*
3. *What do you consider to be the most important social factors in pupil
   typification? Give reasons for your answer.*
4. *Do you think pupils typify teachers? If so, on what basis is this done?
   If not, why not?*

FRATERNISATION: A SURVIVAL STRATEGY FOR THE CLASSROOM

Peter Woods's ethnographic study of Lowfield Secondary School
provides a detailed portrait of school life from the perspective of
teachers and pupils. He studies school processes from an
interactionist perspective and is interested in the way in which
teachers accommodate to school by developing and using survival
strategies which help to alleviate conflict in the classroom. Here,
he discusses one of the strategies he has identified.

Reading 4

'If you can't beat them, join them'

'One of the ways to resolve extreme conflict between
teachers and children is for the teachers to become less adult

and in some sense enter into the world of children. This requires isolating oneself from adult interactions and assuming some of the language and style of children.'

Some staff were

> not altogether sympathetic with the social aims of the school, but fulfilled an informal role which was functional for the school organisation in defusing conflict within the pupil identity of working class children which might otherwise have made it difficult for them to continue in the upper years at the school. As such, these staff acted . . . as a 'safety valve institution', channelling discontent and hostility, while keeping intact the relationship within which the antagonism arises.

> The concern with interest and motivation as exhibited through practical problems in the schools owed as much to the aim of preventing disruption, as to the aim of promoting the inculcation of knowledge.

A prominent *survival strategy* is to work for good relations with the pupils, thus mellowing the inherent conflict, increasing the pupils' sense of obligation, and reducing their desire to cause trouble. It might be thought that this is fairly central to 'progressivist' forms of teaching. But the teachers at Lowfield strongly opposed 'progressivism'. It is taking place therefore within more traditionalist styles.

Fraternization takes many forms. Young teachers, especially, by their appearance, style of dress, manner, speech and interests frequently identify strongly with the pupils. They are often very popular. Implicit alliances can form against the main structure of the school, but, as with teachers of 'backward classes', it can ultimately work in the school's interests, since much bad feeling is defused through this bond with members of staff. On the other hand, of course, pupils with their own survival problem might try to increase their benefits by playing off one teacher against another ('so and so lets us chew in *his* lesson'), so it can promote instability. Older teachers can assume parts of this role. For example, they can display signs of alienation from the official culture, especially where it seeks to dominate. Explicit or implicit disapproval before pupils of a rule or action, especially if perpetrated by the upper hierarchy, is common. In fact it has been suggested that a major function of the head and his deputies is to soak up a lot of the bad feeling in the school, leaving a pleasanter field for front-line teachers and pupils to work in. Some identify with the pupils against outside aspects of the establishment:

> 'I loathe the vicar, who goes up, takes his watch off – and you know you're going to get your twenty minutes' worth – and he says "I've got four points to make" – and he's only done two of them after fifteen minutes . . .'

(Interestingly, this teacher betrays himself before typical secondary modern pupils by identifying with the establishment at all!)

Many teachers share in cultural influences which cross generations. Thus some have recourse to an earthy humour which marks them not as 'a teacher, a man apart', but as 'a man of the people'. Dirty jokes are not excluded, and seem to be particularly appreciated by rebellious male elements in the school. Another shared cultural influence is television. Some lessons I observed abounded in references to popular television programmes, advertisements included. While this might have a pedagogical value, it also has important survival repercussions for the pupils' perceptions of the teacher's identity. Sport also can form a bridge. For example, gangs of adolescent boys follow a football cult. Their discourse consists of jocular abuse directed at others' chosen teams and vigorous championing of one's own at all costs. This aggressive banter is typical of their lifestyle and is indulged in as a form of play. On these terms it is open to teachers, and sometimes they take advantage of it.

Much survival teaching takes the form of entertainment. It is quite often reflected in styles of speech and associated with culture-identification. Thus one teacher I observed employed a local, chatty, pubby style of speech in his teaching, which he indulged to good effect from the control point of view. Another had a cosmopolitan, youthful, 'with-it' style which reinforced his identification with the pupils. Another related almost everything he said to television programmes, making liberal use of standard phrases, and copying situation and character comedy. Less 'identification' associated are forms of teacher wit and humour. A stage manner helps, and the fun is often directed good-naturedly and matily towards the inmates. The displacement of reality in humour neutralizes any potential conflict.

> 'Oh, my God, that smell. Is that that "Brut" again? Open a

window, stand back.' (*Hangs out of window, gasping. Returns to desk.*)

'Oh, my God, those socks!' (*Covers eyes with hand, puts on sun-glasses.*)

'Now who saw *Maxim Gorky* last night? That's the programme you tune into between Mickey Mouse and Long John Silver.'

By this form of humour the teacher retains control and reinforces status. It is a kind of humorous, rather than aggressive, domination technique, but the aggression lurks in the background.

P. Woods, *The Divided School*, 1979, pp. 155–7.

Questions
1. *What do you understand by the term 'survival strategy' (para. 1)?*
2. *What is the role of (i) fraternisation and (ii) humour in the classroom?*
3. *Identify the strategies that are used by teachers and pupils to 'survive' in your classroom.*

BARGAINING FOR MARKS

Examinations, tests and marks are part of the familiar routine of classrooms. In studying an elite independent school for girls in Scotland, Sara Delamont posed basic questions about the way in which the St Luke's pupils handled daily life in the classroom. Here, she demonstrates how pupils use a strategy to gain marks.

Reading 5

Bargaining for marks did go on [in St Luke's] and went hand in hand with discovering how they would be awarded. The best example I collected centred round a geography test. On the third Wednesday of my fieldwork I went to the top geography set. The lesson opened with Mrs Hill being buttonholed by Jill with an involved query about fish farming. Then Mrs Hill called the class to order and announced a test on 'all Scotland' for the following week, giving them the rest of that lesson to revise for it. My notes continue:

A chorus of groans, protests and objections breaks out – dies away – to be replaced by questions on the nature of the test.

Jackie: What type of questions? Short answer or essay?

Mrs Hill: Short answer mostly.

Jill: Why do we have to have tests all the time?

Lorraine: Will we be asked to draw anything?

Karen: Will it be on the board, or are you going to read them out?

Mrs Hill: (Says she'll read them out, and tells them they may have to draw. Then tells them to quieten down or she'll go on to the next topic – Newcastle).

The girls were silenced, and the rest of the period consisted of revision, with girls asking questions about geography as they found points they were not sure of.

The following week I watched the test, which consisted of short answer questions read aloud, such as 'Name two coal-fired power stations in Scotland'. Once it was over the girls swapped papers and marked their neighbour's script.

Mrs Hill: (Announces a firm marking schedule and says there are to be no arguments about it. Then starts asking round the class to get the answers . . .)

Later:

Mrs Hill: Right, now what do we call the area of fertile farmland which includes Perthshire?

(Evelyn is giggling hysterically. Mrs H. asks her what the matter is, but Evelyn does not, or cannot manage to answer. Mrs H. sends her out of the room, takes her test paper away from Angela and makes Angela and Karen swap).

Jackie: The golden girdle.

Karen bursts out laughing, and Mrs H. asks her what is funny.

Karen: Angela has got 'golden griddle', not 'girdle'.

Mrs H. laughs, and the whole class dissolves into laughter.

Mrs H: She can have half a mark for ingenuity. Get Evelyn back in will you?

A chorus of protests about the half mark – for the schedule had stated 'no half marks'.

Mrs H. ignores protests. Tells Evelyn she can see why it was funny, but she should have explained why she was laughing. They go on. Another question asked for 'the

industries of Glasgow after the American War of Inde-
pendence'. After the right answers have been given,
Karen raises her hand and is asked what she wants . . .

Karen: I had 'the slave trade'. Does that count?

Mrs H: That's not an industry.

Karen: Well, for modern Scotland we've got 'tourism' as an
industry – if tourists are an industry surely slaves are too?

Mrs H. gives in and lets her have a half mark too. Another
chorus of 'Not fair' breaks out and is silenced . . . The
next question deals with the potato crop, and Mrs H. says
that only 'early potatoes' will do for the mark – just
'potatoes' won't do. A chorus of protests demand half a
mark for 'potatoes', but Mrs Hill refuses and is adamant.

S. Delamont, *Interaction in the Classroom*, 1983, pp. 105–7.

Questions

1. *What do you understand by the term 'bargaining' (para. 1)?*
2. *Explain the way in which bargains are arrived at between Mrs Hill and her pupils.*
3. *What sociological concepts would you use to analyse what is happening in this classroom?*

ADAPTING RULES

Rules are used by teachers to define their pupils' activities. While
conducting an ethnographic study of a purpose-built coeducational comprehensive school called Bishop McGregor, Robert
Burgess studied the activities that occurred in Newsom classes
where courses were provided for pupils regarded as less willing
and less able. Here, the pupils were involved in redefining
teachers' views.

Reading 6

The headmaster had a series of points of practice for all pupils
which expressed the norms and values of the school. These were
regularly reinforced by the head in his weekly assembly and by
house heads in their assemblies . . . Newsom pupils were confronted with a series of expectations and the penalties involved
for not fulfilling them. While I was at McGregor, smoking was
common among pupils. Teachers regularly saw pupils heading for
the boiler house – the meeting place for pupils who wished to

smoke. To begin with only the location was acknowledged but no evidence of its use was available. However, by the spring term much evidence, in the form of cigarette ends and empty cigarette packets, was scattered around for all to see. When teachers walked up to the boiler house, pupils could be seen smoking, but by the time they arrived all the evidence had disappeared. Most young teachers were tired of existing in a situation where their authority was visibly challenged. They wanted some action taken against the smokers. A petition was therefore circulated by these teachers calling for support from the head and his senior staff. Many signatures were collected and the petition presented to the headmaster. In response, the house heads planned an 'attack' on the smoking area with the result that many smokers were caught and caned.

In the Newsom department there was a different routine. The pupils told me that David Smith (an art teacher who took Newsom classes) did not object to them smoking in his room during lunch breaks. Similarly, Keith Dryden told me that he adapted the no-smoking rule. He explained that he allowed Newsom pupils to go to the toilets for a smoke in the middle of lessons. Furthermore, the pupils told me that Tony Davis smoked in lessons that were held in the workshops and that he did not object if they used his stock cupboard as a place to smoke.

As I had doubts about the authenticity of these stories, I decided to check reports about Newsom teachers who allowed pupils to smoke. When I called on Tony Davis during a Newsom lesson in his workshop, I found him working at a bench with a cigarette balanced carefully on the edge. He would talk to the pupils, take a few 'drags' from his cigarette and return it to the bench. This was not the only smoke in the room. It appeared that some pupils had been smoking.

I found that I could check the smoking stories in my own course. When I took a group of Newsom pupils into the town we had to travel on the local service bus. The pupils boarded an empty bus at the terminus which was some distance from the school. They dashed up to the top deck of the bus and sat in the back seats. I followed and sat just in front of them. As the bus moved off, a boy leaned over my seat with a cigarette in one hand and cigarette lighter in the other. 'Do you mind if I smoke, sir?', he asked. I was uncertain about what to do. I knew the school rules and realized that if I allowed him to smoke I would be breaking the rules. Furthermore, if this was reported to the head by other passengers I would be in trouble and perhaps lose my right to do research. On the other hand, I knew how smoking was treated in the department. To break with this tradition would create problems for my identity as a Newsom teacher. But I was unsure about what staff allowed pupils to do outside the school so I replied, 'You do whatever you would with other Newsom teachers'. 'Thanks very much', he said, lighting his cigarette. Soon the back of the bus was full of smoke as other pupils followed his example. 'You're just like Miss Robinson and Mr Dryden', remarked the pupils. They told me that Sylvia allowed them to smoke when they went on walks and that Keith took them round to his house where they could smoke. However, I still had to check these stories. A few days later when I was talking to Sylvia, I told her what had happened on the bus. The story amused her and she confirmed that smoking regularly occurred when she took pupils out of school. Similarly, Keith also confirmed the story about allowing pupils to smoke. The pupils and staff in the Newsom department had therefore adapted the no-smoking rule.

The no-swearing rule was also adapted. Here, the staff inverted the rule which Goddard had enunciated in an assembly. The head explained that in future he would regard swearing at teachers as seriously as any assault upon their persons. He ended his talk by saying, 'I don't want to be head of a school where people swear at each other'.

I had been the only Newsom teacher in this assembly and so I was asked by my colleagues what Goddard had talked about. When I recounted the story Sylvia laughed and said, 'I'd hate to tell him that he is head of a place where people swear at each other'. I nodded in agreement. I had seen situations in the Newsom department and in my own lessons where arguments occurred between pupils resulting in a considerable amount of swearing. Similar situations were also discussed in many of the diaries that teachers kept for me. They reported that pupils not only swore at each other but also at teachers. Tony Davis's diary indicated that swearing at him and to him was part of the daily routine. In particular he remarked of one class: 'The majority of boys worked on wood carving. Peter Vincent continued on coffee table amidst swearing and bad-tempered outbursts which is normal for the class.' Tony indicated that this behaviour was 'normal' for the class, a point that could be supported on the basis of other conversations I witnessed between Newsom teachers and their pupils. Listening to Keith Dryden talk to two boys one evening, I noticed that he only swore on two occasions but covered it with the phrase, 'oops, that just slipped out' as a means of excusing himself when he swore in front of or at the pupils. This was a linguistic device that I also heard pupils use and which allowed them to swear in the presence of Newsom teachers without fear of sanctions being brought against them.

In these circumstances, Newsom pupils were prepared to redefine the situation. In a conversation with John Slattery, he explained that he had sworn at a teacher:

John   I told Mr Gear to well . . .
RB   What was this?
John   Well we were all supposed to do games last two periods on a Monday, about a couple of months ago. It was really wet so we couldn't go outside and I brought a note in saying I didn't want to do games.
RB   A genuine note?
John   Oh yes, written by me Mam. There was nothing wrong with me though, I just didn't wanna do games and so we all decided we wanted to play table tennis but Mr Gear wouldn't let me play so I said, 'Oh for fuck's sake'. He said, 'Would you mind repeating that?' I said, 'As long as I don't get into trouble'. He said, 'You're chicken' and I said, 'Well as long as I don't get into trouble' and he said 'Go on'. So I said it again and he told me to get out.

This story was an accurate account of what had occurred in the lesson as it was repeated to me in similar terms by the teacher concerned. Despite the change in relationship between the teacher and the pupil further negotiation took place. The pupil was only prepared to repeat the obscenity in return for immunity from punishment. Here, the teacher was ready to comply with the pupil's wishes. The Newsom teachers had redefined the school rule but in turn the pupils had redefined the situation.

R. G. Burgess, *Experiencing Comprehensive Education: A Study of Bishop McGregor School*, 1983, pp. 217–20.

Questions
1. *What do you understand by the concepts 'definition of the situation' and 'redefinition of the situation'?*
2. *Explain the ways in which pupils redefined situations.*

3. *Discuss the ways in which teachers and pupils adapt rules in your school or college. What strategies are involved?*

GENDER IN THE CLASSROOM

How does 'gender' structure classroom situations and how is it structured within them? Michelle Stanworth addressed these questions in a study of seven 'A'-level classes in which she interviewed the teachers and a sample of their male and female pupils. She highlights some of the differences in classroom life for boys and girls.

Reading 7

Boys and girls report the same actions by their teachers, but the interpretations they give to these actions can be very different. The two passages which follow (in response to the only question in the two hour pupil interviews which explicitly refers to gender), illustrate starkly how a teacher's actions can be insulting to girls, but regarded by boys as a trivial matter. Although they share the same classrooms, the experience of classroom life is clearly not the same for girls and boys.

Interviewer: Does it make any difference, do you think, that Mr Macmillan is a man and Mrs Wilson is a woman?

Female pupil: I suppose so, because you think he's a bit of a twit, at least I do. Whereas Mrs Wilson, I suppose I relate to her more because she's a woman.

Interviewer: And do you think she feels the same way, that it's easier for her to relate to girls?

Pupil: Possibly . . . No, I think it's equal actually, the way she relates to boys and girls. But take somebody like Mr Macmillan, he tends to relate better to the boys actually. When he's talking about military history or something like that he says 'I know you ladies won't like this' or something.

Interviewer: I see what you mean. You might feel a little bit as if you'd been excluded from that discussion.

Pupil: Yes, yes. I had another teacher like that at my old school actually. It was really annoying. He kept saying things like – it was in Physics – and he said, 'Now if you were boys you would understand this.' God, ugh! It really annoys me.

Interviewer: Does it make any difference, do you think, that Mr
   Macmillan is a man and Mrs Wilson is a woman?
Male pupil: Possibly, yes. I suppose the men sort of tend
   to . . . be a bit chauvinist, I suppose you could put it, but
   they do that as a joke really. Particularly Mr Macmillan. He
   tends to jokingly separate the two teams really. If it's a sort
   of social rights issue, he'll ask for the point of view of both
   sexes. Or he'll tease the girls that they won't understand
   something, say like military history. But he doesn't really
   concentrate on it.

Whatever the causes of what pupils take to be discriminatory
behaviour on the part of their teachers – and the causes are
undoubtedly complex – the consequences for pupils' views of
themselves must be given serious consideration. As we saw
earlier, small tokens of individual attention are important clues
that pupils go by when deciding whether they are looked on with
favour by their teachers. Because boys are given prominence by
both male and female teachers in classroom activity, they have a
far greater chance of feeling valued. Girls, on the other hand,
who are less often singled out for attention in class, tend to
assume (despite their good marks) that teachers hold them in low
esteem. The girl who described herself as a 'wallpaper person'
was by no means the only one to react in this way to apparent
indifference from teachers.

It is not only the self-images of *individual* pupils which are
shaped by this process. The classroom is one of the few highly
structured environments where adolescent girls and boys
encounter one another on a regular basis, as comparative
strangers. The experiences they have there are an important
source of evaluations of their own, and the other, sex – of their
assessments as to how successfully boys as a group, and girls as a
group, match up to the demands of the adult world. When boys
are more outspoken and manifestly confident – and especially
when teachers take more notice of boys – pupils tend to see this
as evidence that boys in general are more highly valued, and
more capable, than girls.

M. Stanworth, *Gender and Schooling: A Study of Sexual Divisions
in the Classroom*, 1981, pp. 36–7.

Questions
1. *Compare and contrast the boys' and girls' experiences of classroom
   life.*

2. (i) *What different kinds of messages appear to be communicated to boys and girls in school classrooms?* (ii) *Are different messages communicated to boys and girls about (a) their self-image; (b) their educational achievement?*

3. *Consider the way in which 'gender' is used to organise life in your classroom.*

RACE, GENDER AND CLASSROOM BEHAVIOUR

Mary Fuller's data are taken from the study of a multiracial comprehensive school in the London Borough of Brent. She describes a group of black girls who were aware of their double subordination as female and black, but who had adopted a survival strategy of 'going it alone' in which gaining qualifications was important.

Reading 8

As will be clear, acquisition of academic qualifications was an integral part of this sense of control over their future. What was less immediately obvious was the underlying relationship of academic qualifications to the girls' sense of self-worth. In a very real sense they perceived the obtaining of academic qualifications as a public statement of something which they already knew about themselves but which they were also certain was given insufficient public recognition: that they were capable, intelligent, and the equal of boys.

> 'I think people trust you more when you're a boy; they say you're more reliable, you're more trustworthy. Because my dad always says that, he says you can take a boy and you can show him a trade, but you can take a girl and the next minute their heads are all filled up with boys, that she just doesn't want to know. So I'm going to show him, you see!' (Beverley)

That is, their sense of self-worth did not derive from the acquisition of academic qualifications nor, in the future, from obtaining a 'good' job; rather their pursuit of these ends was given meaning by their existing knowledge of their own worth and their understanding that this was often denied. During interviews most of the girls said they thought boys considered themselves superior to girls, an idea which they viewed with amused disbelief or scepticism.

'Most West Indian boys definitely aren't going to let a
woman dominate them or tell them what to do, they firmly
believe that they're the boss and she has to do everything . . . They just have this thing that they are the superior
ones and women are inferior. This equality business – I don't
think that it would ever work in the West Indies, don't think
they'd accept it, might here. And I don't think the West
Indian boys growing up here, I don't think they're going to
accept it either because they always talk about it as a load of
rubbish anyway, because as far as they're concerned they're
superior and they're not going to be equal with a woman, or
anything like that.' (Christa)

The written word does not readily convey the tone in which
Christa spoke, but what was clear was that she, together with
most of the other girls, did not take it as self-evident that males
were superior or deserved to be taken more seriously than,
herself.

To this point in their careers the girls' confidence appeared
well-founded; they had passed a greater number of 'O' level and
CSE exams, and at rather higher grades than had the black boys.
The black girls achieved a mean of 7.6 passes at this level
compared with 5.6 for the black boys, an achievement which put
them second only to Asian boys in performance in 'O' level and
CSE. Similarly, while all the girls had remained in full-time
education for at least one year beyond the statutory school-
leaving age, only two of the black boys had done so. Where girls
had left school or college to take up employment, all mentioned
that they were also continuing their education by day release or
block release schemes or by attending college in the evenings;
only one boy mentioned that he was continuing his education in
any way.

So far the picture drawn seems to be that of the girls as
archetypal 'good' pupils – ones who have high aspirations and
achieve well in public examinations – but this was far from the
truth in most other aspects of their lives in school. Unlike other
pupils who were similarly pro-education, the black girls were not
pro-school. That is to say, their intolerance of the daily routines
and their criticisms of much that went on inside the school were
marked. They shared with some other pupils a view of school as
'boring', 'trivial' and 'childish', and yet at the same time were
markedly different from these same pupils in that they had high

aspirations and a high degree of academic success. Despite their critical view of school the black girls did not define it as 'irrelevant' (as did other pupils who found school boring, etc.), because of the particular importance which they attached to academic achievement. Quine (1974) discusses a similar orientation among the boys in his study of two Midland comprehensive schools.

Most high aspirers and achievers in the school were concerned to demonstrate their seriousness of purpose to teachers and other pupils by certain kinds of classroom behaviour; punctuality, a modicum of attention to lesson content, and a 'respectful' (by no means always deferential) attitude towards teachers, in addition to actually doing the work set. Whether they actively courted a good reputation in other ways or not, such pupils tended to be seen as 'good' pupils. The reverse of this behaviour was taken by both teachers and pupils to indicate a lack of interest in school and was associated with a reputation as a 'bad' pupil.

The black girls conformed to the stereotypes of the good pupil only in so far as they worked conscientiously at the schoolwork or homework set. But they gave all the appearances in class of not doing so, and in many other ways displayed an insouciance for the other aspects of the good pupil role. They neither courted a good reputation among teachers nor seemed to want to be seen as 'serious' by the staff or other pupils. Eschewing behaviour which would bring them into serious conflict with teachers (for example, truanting, direct challenges to a teacher's authority, grossly disruptive behaviour within the classroom), the girls were frequently involved in activities which exasperated the staff and which were yet not quite clearly misdemeanours requiring comment or action on their part. The following examples drawn from field notes represent incidents which occurred with some frequency: openly engaging in some 'illegitimate' activity (reading a magazine, chatting, doing homework for another subject) so that it appeared that the girls were not listening or not working, yet when questioned by the teacher they could show that they had, in fact, taken in what had been said or had actually completed the work assigned; arriving technically late for a lesson but actually seconds before the teacher, who could see their late arrival; handing in work for marking when it suited them rather than immediately it was asked for; complying with a teacher's request somewhat slowly and with a show of complete uninterest, and so on. Studying delinquent pupils (some of them black) in an

American high school, Werthman (1963) describes somewhat similar behaviour. Neither meek and passive nor yet aggressive, and obviously confrontationist in their stance towards teachers, the girls were something of a puzzle to some of their peers and teachers.

Three themes emerged in their discussions of the stance they adopted within school. First, to be seen as a 'good' pupil, i.e., showing too much eagerness in class, appearing to take school too seriously, risked the discovery of their academic and job ambitions and consequently invited ridicule and possibly more from those peers with whom the girls most frequently compared themselves – black boys.

> 'I find that most boys do have ambitions but they're influenced by their friends, so they never get put into practice anyway . . . I think the girls are more ambitious but if they want to do something they don't feel embarrassed about it except when boys, when they hear you're doing 'O' levels, they won't come out with it and say you're a snob but they treat you a bit differently and you can feel it . . . I think West Indian girls might feel a bit funny about that.' (Joan)

> 'I've always got my head in a book. I don't think they [boys in school] like it because they are always commenting on it and they say "You won't get anywhere", and sometimes I think they don't want me to learn or something like that, you know; but I spoke to my mum about it, and she said I shouldn't listen and I should keep working hard.' (Marcia)

In this way their classroom behaviour may be seen as a conscious smoke-screen to confuse others and enable the girls to retain the friendship of their peer group without giving up their aspirations.

Second, to be viewed by teachers as a 'good' pupil was inconsistent with the girls' own view of themselves. 'Good' pupils were boring, were unable to have 'fun', and were in other respects 'immature'. To behave in class like them would invite comparison with people from whom the girls expressly distanced themselves.

Third, the girls believed that other highly aspiring pupils placed too great an emphasis on teachers' opinions in relation to pupils' success: in so far as public examinations were marked by people who did not know the candidates personally, pupils could expect to pass exams on the quality of their work rather than on the quality of their relationship with the teachers who taught them. Very few other pupils discussed pupil–teacher relationships in this way.

The black girls' behaviour within the classroom is, I suggest, intimately connected with their positive identity as black and female. It seems reasonable to suppose that in coming to a sense of their own worth the girls had learnt to rely on their own rather than others' opinion of them. Their weighing up of the potential relevance and importance of teachers was part of a more general stance towards others. The girls were relatively sophisticated in judging who did and did not matter in their pursuit of academic qualifications, for example, so that one could say they adopted a somewhat 'strategic' political stand in relation to other people, including whites generally and white authority in school specifically.

To some extent this can also be seen in their social relationships with other pupils. The girls appeared to treat poor relationships as a resource of essentially individualistic achievement aims rather than as a source of pleasure and/or confirmation in its own right. The girls came together as a result of each of them trying to cope with the difficulties of proving their own worth. This was to be expressed through the acquisition of paper qualifications, not through the living out of a particular peer-based life-style. In a sense the confirmation of the girls' sense of identity could not come from either their peer group or from adults, but only from their own efforts. For this reason the sub-culture was not a readily discernible entity, marked out from others by a particular and visible style. Or rather their style was not the raison d'être of their coming together.

M. Fuller, 'Black girls in a London comprehensive school', in R. Deem (ed), *Schooling for Women's Work*, 1980, pp. 59–61.

Questions
1. *What social factors influence the roles the pupils take in the classroom?*
2. *One girl indicates that she is being pulled in different directions by her mother and her peers. List the ways in which conflict may occur between the peer group and the home.*
3. *What sociological concepts could be used to desribe and interpret the classroom strategies of the black girls?*

ESSAY QUESTIONS

1. To what extent are pupils and teachers free to negotiate their own roles in classrooms? (JMB, 1981)
2. What do you understand by the term 'strategy'? Discuss the ways in which teachers and pupils utilise strategies in the classroom.
3. Examine the strengths and weaknesses of the interactionist approach to schooling.
4. Critically evaluate the sociological evidence on *either* deviance in classrooms *or* sexual divisions in classrooms.

FURTHER READING

Students should consult the books and papers from which the extracts have been taken together with the suggestions for further reading at the end of the previous chapter as many of the studies contain relevant material on classrooms.

1. R. G. Burgess, 'The practice of sociological research: some issues in school ethnography' in R. G. Burgess (ed), *Exploring Society*, British Sociological Association, 1982, pp. 115–35.
   A brief account of the way in which the research was done for the writer's *Experiencing Comprehensive Education*.
2. R. G. Burgess (ed), *The Research Process in Educational Settings: Ten Case Studies*, Falmer Press, 1984.
   Discussions by Stephen Ball, Sara Delamont and Mary Fuller among others on how their studies were done in schools and classrooms.
3. S. Delamont, *Sex Roles and the School*, Methuen, 1980.
   Illustrates the ways in which gender is routinely handled in the classroom.
4. S. Delamont, *Interaction in the Classroom*, 2nd edn, Methuen, 1983.
   A basic guide to sociological research on classroom life including accounts of the perspectives of teachers and pupils.
5. S. Delamont (ed), *Readings in Classroom Interaction*, Methuen, 1984.
   A companion volume to the text on classroom interaction, containing a range of British and American readings.
6. M. Hammersley and P. Woods (eds), *The Process of Schooling*, Routledge and Kegan Paul, 1976.
   Includes papers devoted to theory and method as well as central issues on classroom interaction.
7. D. H. Hargreaves (ed), 'Classroom Studies', *Educational Analysis*, vol. 2, no. 2 (1980) 1–93.
   A special issue of the journal that contains reviews of systematic observation, ethnographic work and sociolinguistic studies of classrooms.

8. P. Woods (ed), *Teacher Strategies*, Croom Helm, 1980.

A collection of papers that focus on teacher activities including the teacher role and teacher commitment.

9. P. Woods (ed), *Pupil Strategies*, Croom Helm, 1980.

A collection of papers about the ways in which pupils cope with school.

10. P. Woods, *Sociology and the School: An Interactionist Viewpoint*, Routledge and Kegan Paul, 1983.

Contains a review of the main interactionist work on schools. It focuses on such concepts as situation, perspective, culture, strategy, negotiation and career.

7
The school curriculum

The beginning of the 1970s heralded the development of the 'new' sociology of education that took as its central problem questions about the 'management of knowledge'. In particular, it was argued by Michael F. D. Young (1971) that sociologists had taken educators' categories and concepts for granted with the result that numerous assumptions were made about knowledge and the content of the curriculum. He argued that sociologists should develop their own concepts and categories and pose questions about the ways in which educational knowledge is selected, organised and stratified within the educational system. The result was that sociologists came closer to examining the content of education and to addressing the question: what counts as 'education'?

Much of the early work that took place within this field of study concerned theoretical analyses which are reflected in the writings of Young, Bernstein and Bourdieu. It was Young who established the critical stance that sociologists might take in studying the school curriculum, while Bernstein (1971) outlined a framework in which he distinguished between different elements of educational knowledge. First, Bernstein considers there is the curriculum which defines what counts as valid knowledge. Secondly, there is pedagogy which is concerned with the transmission of knowledge and which in turn defines what counts as the valid transmission of knowledge. Thirdly, he argues there is evaluation which defines what counts as a valid realisation of this knowledge by those who are taught. In turn, he maintains that it is through these three message systems that the transmission of educational knowledge occurs. Meanwhile, for Bourdieu, education is defined as a system of thought and the educational process is seen as the transmission of culture. However, as Lawton has argued, if the curriculum is defined as a selection from culture, a crucial question concerns *who* selects.

This range of theoretical issues has taken much of the sociologist's attention, with the result that selection and stratification have become key concerns in the study of the school curriculum. Indeed, Bernstein summed up some of the central issues involved in the sociological study of the curriculum when he stated 'how a society selects, classifies, distributes, transmits and evaluates the educational knowledge it considers to be public, reflects both the distribution of power and the principles of social control' (1971, p. 47). While much theoretical interest has been shown in these issues there has been relatively little empirical work on these themes.

Nevertheless, sociologists have taken a critical stance towards official reports and government documents that discuss the school curriculum with the result that there has been much interest in questions of control. In particular, sociologists have considered the extent to which central government, local government and teachers have control of the curriculum. Lawton, for example, has used both historical and contemporary documentary material to address such questions in the English educational system, while other researchers have focused on the school to look at the characteristics associated with school subjects and the way in which subjects become established (Goodson and Ball, 1984).

Such work only relates to the official curriculum. Accordingly, sociologists have also looked at other elements of learning that take place within school and which are referred to as the 'hidden curriculum'. This aspect of the curriculum includes a range of messages that are transmitted to pupils about the rules, routines and regulations associated with classroom life.

The readings that have been included in this chapter reflect some of the main themes in this area of study. We begin with Michael Young, who identifies some of the key issues that sociologists need to address when studying curricula. Secondly, we turn to an analysis of the stratification of the curriculum and of knowledge within the English educational system (as advocated by the Norwood Committee) and within a comprehensive school as shown by Nell Keddie. Thirdly, we focus on the process of becoming a school subject using case study material from Ivor Goodson's work and the distinction between academic and non-academic subjects using Robert Burgess's ethnographic description of a non-academic area of the school curriculum. The readings that follow turn our attention to the hidden curriculum of schooling. David Hargreaves and Judy Samuel provide evidence on the lessons that can be learned from woodwork and science classes respectively, besides the subjects at hand. Finally, statistical data from the Department of Education and Science provide some trends on the availability and choice of subjects among fourth and fifth form pupils which relates to the official, as well as the hidden curriculum of schooling.

Sociologists who have been concerned with the study of the curriculum have considered such issues as: what knowledge is available in the classroom? What are the characteristics of school knowledge? How is knowledge transmitted? To whom is knowledge transmitted and for what purpose? In turn, they have also posed a number of questions about school subjects such as: what subjects are selected? Who selects subject knowledge? What versions of subjects are transmitted in the classroom? Further questions have also been raised about the hidden messages of the curriculum and the way they are transmitted in the classroom. But despite all this activity, sociologists have yet to relate the 'principles of selection and organization that underlay curricula to their institutional and interactional setting in schools and classrooms and to the wider social structure' (Young, 1971, p. 24).

THE SOCIOLOGY OF KNOWLEDGE AND THE STUDY OF THE CURRICULUM

The sociological perspective that has dominated the study of the curriculum has been derived from the sociology of knowledge. Writing in the early 1970s, Michael F. D. Young discusses the way in which this perspective may be used to pose questions and challenge assumptions about the school curriculum.

Reading 1

Consideration of the assumptions underlying the selection and organization of knowledge by those in positions of power may be a fruitful perspective for raising sociological questions about curricula. We can make this more explicit by starting with the assumptions that those in positions of power will attempt to define what is to be taken as knowledge, how accessible to different groups any knowledge is, and what are the accepted relationships between different knowledge areas and between those who have access to them and make them available. It is thus the exploration of how these processes happen, since they tend in other than pre-literate societies to take place in and through educational institutions, that should form the focus of a sociology of education. Our understanding of the processes is so rudimentary at present, that it is doubtful if we can postulate any clear links between the organization of knowledge at the level of social structure and the process as it involves teachers in classrooms. However, from these assumptions we can, drawing on Bernstein, pose three interrelated questions about how knowledge is organized in curricula.

1.) The power of some to define what is 'valued' knowledge leads to problems of accounting for how 'stratified' knowledge is and by what criteria. Implicit in this idea of '*stratification of knowledge*' is the distinction between the 'prestige' and the 'property' components of stratification. To the former are linked the different social evaluations placed on different knowledge areas, and to the latter are the notions of 'ownership' and freedom (or restriction of access). Thus the 'property' aspect of stratification points to 'knowledge' in use, and the reward structure associated with it. It suggests that in different societies the dominant conception of knowledge may be akin to 'private property', property shared by particular groups, or communally available on the analogy of 'common land'. The analysis which follows implicitly places greater emphasis on the prestige component of the stratification of knowledge. This is in part because the focus of the analysis is on curricula in one society rather than across societies, when it would become easier to conceptualize different definitions of 'knowledge as property'.

2.) The restriction of the accessibility of knowledge areas to different groups, poses the question in relation to curricula as to what is the *scope* of curricula available to different age groups, and more specifically to the social factors influencing the degree and kind of specialization at any age level.

3.) Earlier in the paper I raised the question as to what fields of enquiry were, at different times and in different cultures, embraced by a term like 'science'. More broadly this raises the question of the relation between knowledge areas and between those with access to them.

> M. F. D. Young, 'An approach to the study of curricula as socially organised knowledge', in M. F. D. Young (ed), *Knowledge and Control: New Directions for the Sociology of Education*, 1971, pp. 31–2.

Questions
1. *What sociological perspectives can be used to pose questions about the curriculum?*
2. *What do you understand by the term 'stratification of knowledge' (para. 2)?*
3. *To what extent is knowledge socially distributed among different groups in your school or college? Give examples to illustrate your answers.*

THREE TYPES OF SECONDARY SCHOOLS . . . THREE TYPES OF CURRICULUM

Although the 1944 Education Act established the tripartite system of secondary education in England and Wales, the organisation and curriculum arrangements had already been advocated in the Spens Report in 1938 and in the Norwood Report in 1943. The following statement from the Norwood

Committee provided a blueprint for the secondary school curriculum for some years.

Reading 2

Types of Curriculum

In a wise economy of secondary education pupils of a particular type of mind would receive the training best suited for them and that training would lead them to an occupation where their capacities would be suitably used; that a future occupation is already present to their minds while they are still at school has been suggested, though admittedly the degree to which it is present varies. Thus, to the three main types sketched [earlier in the report] there would correspond three main types of curriculum, which we may again attempt to indicate.

First, there would be a curriculum of which the most characteristic feature is that it treats the various fields of knowledge as suitable for coherent and systematic study for their own sake apart from immediate considerations of occupation, though at a later stage grasp of the matter and experience of the methods belonging to those fields may determine the area of choice of employment and may contribute to success in the employment chosen.

The second type of curriculum would be closely, though not wholly, directed to the special data and skills associated with a particular kind of occupation; its outlook and its methods would always be bounded by a near horizon clearly envisaged. It would thus be closely related to industry, trades and commerce in all their diversity.

In the third type of curriculum a balanced training of mind and body and a correlated approach to humanities, Natural Science and the arts would provide an equipment varied enough to enable pupils to take up the work of life: its purpose would not be to prepare for a particular job or profession and its treatment would make a direct appeal to interests, which it would awaken by practical touch with affairs.

Of the first it may be said that it may or may not look forward to University work; if it does, that is because the Universities are traditionally concerned with the pursuit of knowledge as such. Of the second we would say that it may or may not look forward to the Universities, but that it should increasingly be directed to advanced studies in so far as the Universities extend their orbit in response to the demands of the technical branches of industry.

> C. Norwood, *Curriculum and Examinations in Secondary Schools*, 1943, p. 4.

Questions

1. *What arrangements are suggested by the Norwood Committee for providing different kinds of curricula for different pupils?*
2. *What assumptions are made about the purposes of the secondary school curriculum?*
3. *To what extent has this statement on the secondary school curriculum acted as a blueprint for English secondary education since the Second World War?*

THE SOCIAL DISTRIBUTION OF CLASSROOM KNOWLEDGE

Nell Keddie's study of the humanities department in a comprehensive school in the early 1970s provides an analysis of the social distribution of classroom knowledge and the process of differentiation in the school curriculum. Her study raises questions about classroom processes and the ways in which knowledge is transmitted.

Reading 3

'I envisage problems with 4Cs in understanding unusual relationships. The meaning of relationships, it's going to be very difficult to get this over to them.' (Teacher J)

'Yes, um, when we did it with the 4Cs before they, er, didn't seem particularly interested that, er, other people had family groups of their own. Because it wasn't real to them, it was so far removed, it didn't seem of complete . . . of any relevance to them.' (Teacher L)

'I think if you're dealing with it purely in terms of kinship diagrams and white sheets, again you're actually reducing the interest again, if you make it too intellectual. What illustrative material is there on this? . . . I think I've said this before . . . that sociology has its validity in its abstractions and in its intellectual [untranscribable] . . . to what extent the 4Cs will take that or to what extent it will remain a series of stories about families . . .' (Teacher J – not himself a sociologist)

The picture that emerges from these comments which are highly representative, is one of oppositions that describe material and pupils: 'intellectual' is opposed to 'real', and 'abstractions' to 'stories'. One teacher implies that so long as the material is accessible only in terms of kinship diagrams and buff cards it will be too 'intellectual'. To make it 'real', illustrative material is needed. The points they make are not ones simply of method, but are about methods relating to C stream pupils, and so questions arise not only about why C pupils are believed to need non-intellectual material, but also why A pupils are believed not to need illustrative material and not to have problems in understanding 'the meaning of relationships'. The suggestion in these comments is that there is something in the material which 'it might be possible to bring out with the As'. The phrases 'bring it out', 'make explicit', the 'implications of moral problems', 'economic implications', seem to point to a range of understanding that is not available to C pupils who can engage only marginally with the material. Teacher J provides a further gloss on this when he says after a lesson with a C group:

'This stuff [on language] is much too difficult for them . . . On the other hand they could cope with the family stuff. They could say something in their own words about different kinds of family, because they already knew something about them even if they did not know the correct term.'

'The correct term' implies something about how status may be attributed to knowledge. The pupils' ignorance of the 'correct term' suggests their deficiency. In the following discussion it is further suggested that the range of understanding that is available to C stream pupils must be rooted in their 'experience', and that this is linked with another phrase teachers often use about adapting teaching material for C pupils: 'putting it in language they can understand':

TEACHER J: How about the family for the Cs? It may have more in it for them because it's nearer home.

TEACHER B: There'll be a lot of visual stimulus for discussion . . . The Cs should be able to get somewhere with discussion . . . we won't do the history of the family with them, it's too difficult, probably too difficult for anyone.

What seems to emerge overall from the way teachers discuss teaching material in relation to pupils' abilities is an assumption that C pupils cannot master subjects: both the 'abstractions of sociology' and the 'economic implications' are inaccessible to them. The problem then in teaching C pupils is that you cannot teach them subjects. When A pupils do subjects it can be assumed by teachers that they do what, in terms of the *subject*, is held to be appropriate, and material is prepared with regard to what is seen as the demands of the *subject*. In teaching C pupils modifications must be made with regard to the *pupil*, and it is as though the subject is scanned for or reduced to residual 'human elements' or a 'series of stories'.

> N. Keddie, 'Classroom knowledge', in M. F. D. Young (ed), *Knowledge and Control: New Directions for the Sociology of Education*, 1971, pp. 147–8.

Questions
1. *How do the teachers intend modifying materials for 'C' stream pupils?*
2. *What is the relationship between social status and types of school knowledge?*
3. *To what extent do the teachers' accounts suggest that pupils are stratified by classroom knowledge?*

BECOMING A SCHOOL SUBJECT

Ivor Goodson has conducted a series of historical case studies to examine the ways in which different subjects (biology, geography and rural studies) establish a place in the school curriculum. He examines patterns of conflict and change in the process of becoming a school subject, taking geography as an example in the following reading.

Reading 4

The establishment of geography – 'how geography was rendered a discipline' – was a protracted, painstaking and fiercely contested process. The story is not one of the translation of an academic discipline devised by ('dominant') groups of scholars in universities into a pedagogic version to be used as a school subject. Rather, the story unfolds in reverse order and can be seen as a drive from low-status groups at school level to progressively colonise areas within the university sector – thereby earning the right for scholars in the new field to define knowledge that could be viewed as a discipline. The process of evolution for school subjects can be seen not as a pattern of disciplines 'translated' down or of 'domination' downwards but very much as a process of 'aspiration' upwards.

To summarise the stages in the evolution of geography: these offer some support for Layton's tentative model although they indicate the existence of a stage preceding his stage one. In this stage, teaching was anything but 'messianic', for the subject was taught by non-specialists and comprised a 'dreary collection of geographical facts and figures'. The threshold for 'take-off' on the route to academic establishment began with MacKinder's remarkably successful and sustained recipe for the subject's promotion drawn up in 1903. The strategy reads very much like trade union pleas for the closed shop: In this case the pressure group in question was of course the Geographical Association. In the MacKinder manifesto the geography teacher is to set the exams and is to choose exams that are best for the 'common acceptation' of the subject, the teaching of geography is to be exclusively in the hands of trained geographers and the universities are to be encouraged to establish schools of geography 'where geographers can be made'.

The strategy offered solutions for the major problems geography faced in its evolution. Most notable of these was the idiosyncratic and information-based nature of school geography. Initially the subject stressed personal, pedagogic and utilitarian arguments for its inclusion in curricula: 'We seek to train future citizens', and moreover a citizen 'must have a topographical background if he is to keep order in the mass of information which accumulates in the course of his life' (1919). Later the subject was advocated because 'travel and correspondence have now become general' (1927). But the result of these utilitarian and pedagogic emphases was that comments arose as to the 'expansiveness' of the subject and the fact that it became 'more and more to be a "world citizenship"' (1930s).

The problem was that identified by MacKinder in 1903; geographers needed to be 'made' in the universities then the piecemeal changes in pursuit of school relevance could be controlled and directed. The growth of the subject in the schools provided an overwhelming argument for the subject to be taught in the universities. As Wooldridge noted later: 'It has been conceded that if geography is to be taught in schools it must be learned in universities'. Slowly, therefore, a uniformity in the subject was established to answer those who observed the chameleon nature of the subject's knowledge structure. Alice Garnett noted that it was not until after 1945 that most school departments of geography were directed by specialist-trained geographers, but as a result of this training 'most of the initial marked differences and contrasts in subject personality had been blurred or obliterated'.

The definition of geography through the universities instead of the schools began to replace the pedagogic or utilitarian bias with arguments for academic rigour: and as early as 1927 Hadow had contended that 'the main objective in good geographical teaching is to develop, as in the case of history, an attitude of mind and mode of thought characteristic of the subject'. However, for several decades university geography was plagued both by the image of the subject as essentially for school children and by the idiosyncratic interpretations of the various university departments, especially in respect to fieldwork. Thus while establishment in universities solved the status problems of the subject within schools, within universities themselves the subject's status still remained low. The launching of 'new geography' with aspirations to scientific or social scientific rigour is therefore partly to be understood as a strategy for finally establishing geography's status at the highest level. In this respect the current position of the subject in universities would seem to confirm the success of new geography's push for parity of esteem with other university disciplines.

> I. F. Goodson, *School Subjects and Curriculum Change*, 1982, pp. 82–3.

Questions

1. *What are the main stages in the evolution of geography as an academic subject?*
2. *What social factors do you think have influenced the development of geography as an academic subject?*
3. *In what ways does your school/college distinguish between academic, non-academic and practical subjects?*

NOT A 'PROPER' SUBJECT?

Robert Burgess considers subject status while discussing the curriculum with a group of comprehensive school pupils who were regarded by their teachers as the 'less willing' and the 'less able'. In the school he studied they were called Newsom pupils who were provided with a Newsom course which was defined as 'non-academic'.

Reading 5

In Newsom, not even the subject areas were recognizable. New titles had been substituted with the idea of making courses more 'practical', more 'relevant', more vocationally orientated and to include some elements of choice. However, as we shall see, the pupils were critical of what was on offer.

The Newsom Report had indicated the importance of subject labels as it stated:

> A subject name is not only a signpost to the pupils of what a lesson will be about, it also provides a similar reminder to the teacher. It marks out in intelligible shorthand the kind of contribution he is to make to the educational programme. It also links this contribution with his own adult field of knowledge. He speaks with more conviction in this field. When he is on his own ground, his pupils should feel that this lesson is not just textbook stuff. (Newsom, 1963, p. 125)

As far as subjects were concerned, these were no longer visible in the course titles given to pupils. The knowledge that was transmitted included simplified versions of subject material and commonsense knowledge that the teachers considered would be relevant to 16-year-olds who would leave school without taking many examinations. For the pupils this was perceived as very low status. Indeed, many of the pupils talked about 'doing nothing' in their classes which they compared with real learning that had taken place in subject classes in earlier years. In a conversation with Sheila Brown, Jenny Nelson and Sarah Molinski, these comparisons were continually made. Sheila and Jenny summed up the situation as follows:

Jenny: My best year here [at McGregor School], I thought was my first year. It was really great.
Sheila: Yes. Geography, English, Maths, tutorial, R.E. You learnt loads here you know. It would be great if it went through all the years.

Jenny and Sarah: Yes.

Sheila: Yes you could learn the whole lot, never mind what anybody else wanted to do.

Jenny: I get very fed up when I'm sitting at home and I think well why do I have to do this Newsom?

Sheila: Yes.

Jenny: I sometimes even cry because I get that depressed about it.

Indeed, Jenny considered that they were were no longer taking subjects like geography and history where *real* learning took place.

This view was also shared by the boys who also saw Newsom as 'doing nothing'. This view was summed up in a conversation with Terry Nicholls who compared Newsom adversely with work in examination groups.

RB: You do nothing?

Terry: No not much.

RB: Surely you do something?

Terry: No just sit around and do woodcarving. I also do Art but well Art's taking a CSE.

Malcolm: Well you done a lot in Newsom in the fourth year didn't you? Cooking and woodwork and metalwork.

Terry: I didn't do metalwork. I got chucked out. I don't reckon much to Newsom but the rest of the school is all right. If you're taking an 'O' level course it's all right. The teachers are pretty good then but when you're in Newsom it's just a mess around. It's a wasted two years.

RB: Why is it a wasted two years?

Terry: Because I'm achieving nothing am I? You come to school to achieve something like the kids trying to get their 'O' levels and their CSE's while we are just sitting around watching the world go by.

In these terms, Newsom courses were criticized as not involving learning and not providing opportunities for pupils to achieve in comparison with subject courses in earlier years and examination courses in the fourth and fifth years. In turn, some girls complained that the practical courses that were on offer in woodcarving, jewellery making and building were 'boys courses' that were not of interest to them. The boys also complained of boredom and about courses that the teachers considered would be relevant to them. Patrick McConnell presented this perspective:

Patrick: The kids in Newsom complain how bored they are and how they want to do something interesting and the teachers say, 'right we'll do something about banking'. The things they do about it are just no good to us. They're going to do us no good when we leave anyway.

RB: Why not?

Patrick: Well the things they teach us, like this decorating or say that Money Matters. You do how to spend your money. Now they told you, they kinda told you, showed you, how to buy a house, decorate it and insure it and all that kinda stuff you know. But the way they taught it, the way they taught you how to do it you'd either have to be a mathematician or a multi-millionaire.

In this respect, classes which were perceived by the teachers as practical, relevant and vocationally orientated were defined by the pupils as boring. For them Newsom classes and subject classes in the core curriculum (that were seen by many teachers as really further Newsom groups) had little to offer. As a consequence classes were missed, whole days were taken off school and attempts were made by pupils and teachers to modify the activities that occurred within classes.

R. G. Burgess, 'It's not a proper subject: it's just Newsom', in I. F. Goodson and S. J. Ball (eds), *Defining the Curriculum*, 1984, pp. 190–2.

Questions
1. *What characteristics did the pupils associate with 'proper subjects'?*
2. *What constituted 'doing nothing'?*
3. *What had the pupils learned from the Newsom courses?*

LESSONS FROM WOODWORK

Sociologists have not only focused on the 'official curriculum' but also on other aspects of schooling that transmit messages to pupils. It is this aspect of schooling that has become known as the 'hidden curriculum'. In reflecting on his school experience, David Hargreaves discusses some lessons he learned in woodwork classes.

Reading 6

Most teachers have little personal experience of systematic failure; as pupils they were almost always relatively successful – though they are anxious to tell us that they too were rebels in their own way. Some, like me, have a skeleton or two in their academic cupboard. I was not successful, during my schooldays, at woodwork. Slowly I grew to dislike and then to hate the subject at which I was failing; and so, not surprisingly, what few skills I had deteriorated rapidly. Soon I was a target of teacher criticism. 'Everyone stop work', the teacher would announce, 'and look at Hargreaves.' I knew I was to be the exemplar of what not to be doing. Naturally I gave up woodwork at the earliest opportunity and forgot about it. When I grew up and bought a home, I found I needed to re-hang a door; suddenly long-forgotten phantoms from my woodwork lessons besieged my mind. My hands trembled as I bought my Black and Decker tools in the shop. Not until I had successfully completed the work did I dispel my fears and sense of incapacity. But with my renewed feelings of competence came another realization, that I had been able to consign my experiences in woodwork to distant corners of my subconscious only because in most of my other school subjects I had been relatively successful. My conspicuous failure had been drowned in a sea of moderate success. Suppose, however, my failure had not been confined to woodwork lessons; suppose that experience had been replicated in art and music, in French and physics, in English and mathematics: what then? For the first time in my life I realized how little I understood what a persistent experience of failure in school could mean to a pupil. Even now I am not sure that I can perform that feat of imagination required to put myself in the shoes of such a pupil.

The nearest I can come is to imagine a school in which the aspects in which I was least successful (the physical–manual) replace those aspects in which I was most successful (the cognitive–intellectual). In this nightmare my secondary school's timetable is dominated by periods of compulsory woodwork and metalwork, gymnastics, football and cricket, drawing and painting, technical drawing, swimming and cross-country running. Sandwiched between these lessons, but only in thin slices, appear welcome lessons in arithmetic and English, in French and history. Some of these, however, cease to be available to me after the third year; they clash with the more important subjects of technical drawing and gymnastics which I need for higher education and a good job. I enjoy most lessons very little; I am bored and make little effort in areas where I seem destined to fail. The temptation to 'muck about' in lessons, and even to truant, is almost irresistible. My friends soon matter to me much more than anything else in school and our greatest pleasure is in trying to subvert and mock the institution which we are forced to attend for five long years. I don't think my teachers, who seem so strong and so clever with their hands and feet, really understand me at all. Quite often they are kind, but I know they look down on me and think it's all rather hopeless in my case. I'll be glad to leave school.

D. H. Hargreaves, *The Challenge for the Comprehensive School: Culture, Curriculum and Community*, 1982, pp. 63–4.

Questions

1. *What messages were transmitted to David Hargreaves in his woodwork lessons?*
2. *What sociological concepts would you use to analyse Hargreaves' school experience?*
3. *What subjects would constitute a 'nightmare timetable' for you? Consider the messages that would be transmitted and the way you would respond to them.*

TEXTBOOK MESSAGES

On the basis of her analysis of science textbooks, Judy Samuel illustrates how the books not only provide information on science but also contribute to discrimination against girls. She provides examples of the language and illustrations that reinforce stereotypical images of women in society.

Reading 7

I feel that in some respects it is very difficult for men physics and chemistry teachers not to discriminate against the girls in their classes, even when they are aware of the possibility of this and have made a conscious decision not to do so. For example, a great many physics and chemistry textbooks (especially those intended for either younger or less able pupils) refer to the student exclusively as 'he' and reinforce the masculinity of the subject through the pictures they use. In these circumstances it is hardly surprising that many male teachers use these same masculine terms uncritically. A few examples will illustrate how the message is conveyed to both the teacher and the pupils.

1. The Nuffield chemistry O level handbook (intended for teachers) has eleven photographs of students: eight of boys doing some of the most difficult and interesting experiments in the book, one of girls doing a simple experiment, one of boys watching a demonstration and one of boys and girls watching a film. Both the teachers shown are men.

2. McDuell, a modern book for pupils studying CSE chemistry, has a brightly coloured photograph on the front cover of a boy doing an experiment, and a girl standing behind him recording the results.

3. In Chaplin and Keighley, a text for pupils studying physics to CSE, one of the authors is a woman, and some of the questions mention a girl as well as a boy. Nevertheless the student is referred to as 'he' throughout. The book contains sixteen photographs showing scientists at work, but only two show women; in one, a woman horticulturist is standing behind a male colleague, and one photograph features a woman – she is a nurse!

> J. Samuel, 'Feminism and science teaching: some classroom observations', in A. Kelly (ed), *The Missing Half: Girls and Science Education*, 1981, pp. 252–3.

Questions
1. *How is the hidden curriculum transmitted through the science textbooks?*
2. *What messages are transmitted by the science textbooks about boys and girls and scientific work?*
3. *Examine the textbooks available in any three subjects you are studying. What messages do they convey about the social position of boys and girls?*

CURRICULAR DIFFERENCES FOR BOYS AND GIRLS

There is a range of statistical data that compares the experiences of boys and girls in school subjects and examination performance. In particular, considerable interest has been shown in the availability and choice of subjects among secondary school pupils which will influence patterns of performance and future careers.

Reading 8

Table. *The Availability and Choice of Subject Options by Fourth and Fifth Form Pupils in Single Sex and Mixed Secondary Schools*

		Being offered		Choosing		Taking	
		Single sex	Mixed	Single sex	Mixed	Single sex	Mixed
		Per cent of totals of pupils		Per cent of those to whom offered		Per cent of totals of pupils	
		per cent	per cent	per cent	per cent	per cent	per cent
Physics	Boys	85	91	60	52	51	47
	Girls	62	75	23	15	14	11
Chemistry	Boys	81	79	36	35	29	28
	Girls	75	78	27	22	20	17
Biology	Boys	79	91	39	30	31	27
	Girls	96	96	49	53	47	51
French	Boys	75	87	37	28	28	24
	Girls	92	90	49	43	45	39
German	Boys	33	36	21	11	7	4
	Girls	44	38	18	21	8	8
Geography	Boys	91	61	55	54	50	33
	Girls	72	61	53	46	38	28
History	Boys	92	57	45	40	41	23
	Girls	69	61	46	48	32	29
Art	Boys	97	98	36	38	35	37
	Girls	98	98	39	37	38	36
Music	Boys	55	75	11	13	6	10
	Girls	94	81	16	16	15	13

Department of Education and Science, *Curricular Differences for Boys and Girls*, 1975, Table 7, p. 13.

Questions

1. *Describe the main patterns of subject choice by boys and girls.*
2. *Compare the availability and choice of (i) physics (ii) biology by boys and girls.*
3. *What sociological evidence would you use to account for the choice of subjects by boys and girls?*

ESSAY QUESTIONS

1. Show how insights from the sociology of knowledge can be applied to the study of one area of social life. (AEB, 1983)

2. Every school has a curriculum: subjects offered, and areas of knowledge to be studied. How have sociologists analysed the nature of the curriculum? (JMB, 1980)

3. Does the school curriculum contribute to social inequality?

4. What influence does the 'hidden curriculum' have upon pupil learning?

FURTHER READING

The sociological study of the school curriculum has involved much theoretical rather than empirical study. However, the following suggestions attempt to provide a guide to a range of sociological issues involved in this area of study.

1. Department of Education and Science, *Curricular Differences for Boys and Girls*, HMSO, 1975.

   Provides important source materials that could be the subject of sociological analysis on the 'curriculum' and the 'hidden curriculum'.

2. I. F. Goodson, *School Subjects and Curriculum Change*, Croom Helm, 1982.

   Includes a series of historical case studies on biology, geography and rural studies and discusses the process of becoming a school subject.

3. I. F. Goodson and S. J. Ball (eds), *Defining the Curriculum*, Falmer Press, 1984.

   Includes ethnographic and historical studies on aspects of school subjects.

4. D. H. Hargreaves, *The Challenge for the Comprehensive School: Culture, Curriculum and Community*, Routledge and Kegan Paul, 1982.

   A very clearly written book that includes a sociological analysis of the implications of the curriculum for comprehensive education.

5. A. Kelly (ed), *The Missing Half: Girls and Science Education*, Manchester University Press, 1981.

   A collection of papers that analyse the pattern of girls' under-achievement in science and includes a consideration of curriculum content in science subjects.

6. D. Lawton, *Class, Culture and the Curriculum*, Routledge and Kegan Paul, 1975.

   Provides a useful synthesis of sociological writing and proposes a 'common culture curriculum'.

7. D. Lawton, *The Politics of the Curriculum*, Routledge and Kegan Paul, 1980.

   An analysis of curriculum control with special reference to England and Wales.

8. R. Meighan, *A Sociology of Educating*, Holt Rinehart and Winston, 1981.

   A basic text that includes several interesting chapters on the hidden curriculum of schooling.

9. M. Shipman, *Inside a Curriculum Project*, Methuen, 1974.

   An observational study on the development of a curriculum project.

10. M. F. D. Young (ed), *Knowledge and Control: New Directions for the Sociology of Education*, Collier-Macmillan, 1971.

    A set of papers that stimulated much sociological interest on the study of the curriculum. It contains Basil Bernstein's paper 'On the classification and framing of educational knowledge'.

8

Educational politics and policy-making

In concluding their book *Education, Politics and the State*, Salter and Tapper (1981) comment that 'There is a severe danger that important educational change will take place in Britain unbeknown to many educational sociologists' (p. 221). For they indicate that although sociologists have been interested in the education of the working class, and questions of social and cultural reproduction, they have only indirectly examined political and administrative aspects of educational change. These remarks point to a major gap in sociological study, for relatively little has been written on educational politics and educational policy-making from a sociological perspective.

In the early 1980s, when the educational system is confronted with cuts in public expenditure, falling rolls, curriculum changes – such as the Certificate of Pre-Vocational Education (Joint Board, 1984) – and unemployment, it is essential that the sociology of education examines the social, political and economic effects of educational change by becoming more policy orientated and more politically aware. Sociologists of education need to consider the different political and ideological views that have influenced the decision-making process and directions of educational change. In part, the theoretical perspectives that focus on equality, inequality and social justice can be used to examine educational policy, as can critical accounts of education that have utilised a Marxist, neo-Marxist or feminist perspective. Accordingly, sociologists can turn their attention to politics and policy as well as to social problems, social justice and social change, in relation to education. Among the key questions that sociologists can address are: who participates in educational politics and policy-making? Why do they participate? How do they participate? What aims and objectives are being pursued? What are the effects of educational policy? As with other areas of educational study, the positions that are adopted show considerable variation; different stances are taken depending on the political and ideological positions adopted by the participants.

The readings in this chapter have been selected in an attempt to highlight political and policy issues in relation to educational questions that have been examined in earlier chapters. In turn, they represent different perspectives, and different sets of data over which there has been some debate in the 1970s and early

160

1980s. However, before turning to some of the issues, it is important to identify the parties involved in educational politics and the policy-making process. Janet Finch begins by indicating that it is not enough to focus on educational politics and educational policy at the level of central government, local government or schools. She highlights the importance of pressure groups, interest groups, parents and teachers who all exert influence upon the formal decision-making process. As Finch indicates, the dynamics of such processes can best be understood through an analysis of critical case studies. In her extract, Janet Finch briefly reviews the significance of the events at William Tyndale Junior School for what they can teach us about the relationships between the parties involved in educational decision-making. In a similar vein, many commentators have focused upon the politics of comprehensive education, which can be used to analyse the relationships between central authority, local authority and other groups involved in educational change.

In examining comprehensive education, researchers have worked on matters concerning inequality and equality of educational opportunity (see Chapters 3 and 4). In the reading from Caroline Benn's work we are brought back to consider patterns of inequality but in relation to decisions that have been taken about schools by those who work outside them. Politicians have increasingly looked to research evidence for some guidance on policy issues. On the basis of the social research that arose from the Plowden Report, decisions were taken about over-coming disadvantage by a policy of positive discrimination. Yet such programmes themselves need some evaluation. In this respect, the reading from Mortimore and Blackstone brings us back to curriculum issues (see Chapter 7) but in relation to policy matters concerning positive discrimination that can be used to reflect on the impact of policy on educational practice and provision. In turn, the readings from the work of Barry Troyna and Rosemary Deem consider the influence of policy provision for black pupils and for girls and women respectively. In both extracts we are not only directed towards analysing the political and policy-making process but also to considering the social context in which policy occurs and the ideological stances that are taken.

One area in the late 1970s and early 1980s where different positions can be examined concerns the contributions that sociologists and others have made to the analysis of the 'Great Debate' in education and the relationship between school and work (see Chapter 2). In this chapter, one reading highlights the official position taken in a government document, while another (by John Beck) provides a critique of the initiatives that have followed in the late 1970s and early 1980s as a response to employment and unemployment.

Many of these discussions concerning politics and policy in education have a direct impact on schools, teachers and pupils. It is, therefore, appropriate to turn to an account from Her

Majesty's Inspectors (HMI) on the implications of the cuts for
educational activities and educational resources. Here it is the
sociologist's task to consider the implications that arise from
political decisions and policy initiatives.

This chapter attempts to bring a further dimension to some of
the issues that have been raised not only earlier in this volume
but also in the sociology of education. It is time that sociologists
extended their research on schools and schooling to include the
policy decisions taken in 'the corridors of power' which are
informed by a variety of political and ideological perspectives.

THE DYNAMICS OF EDUCATIONAL POLICY-MAKING

Educational policy-making in the English educational system is
marked by a series of complex interactions between a number of
different groups. In this reading Janet Finch isolates the groups
involved in policy-making and discusses the interpretations
associated with educational policy in England.

Reading 1

[A] brief account of the three levels at which policy is made and
implemented [may concern] the formal distribution of powers
and duties; but the formulation and outcome of 'policy' in any
given instance may also be shaped by interventions from other
sources. At central government level, for example, decisions
taken in the Treasury may sometimes be more important than
those taken in the DES, especially in an era of public expenditure
cuts. Media interventions, which focus public attention on a
particular aspect of educational provisions at a given time, can
significantly influence decisions taken within the formal structure.
Pressure groups and interest groups of various sorts (representing
teachers or parents, for example) sometimes make quite
successful interventions in the policy-making process. For
example, the National Union of Teachers was active in the 1960s
and 1970s in pressing for comprehensive plans to be developed at
local level, and in pressing for them to be approved by the DES
after the Conservatives had returned to office in 1970.

Parents are a group whose potential capacity for intervening
successfully has been increased since 1980. Under the 1944 Act
they have the duty to ensure that their children receive full-time
education, and the LEA has the duty, wherever possible, to
ensure that children are educated in accordance with the wishes
of their parents. The 1980 Act accorded them the right of
representation on governing bodies for the first time. Probably

much more important in terms of the impact which parents *actually* are likely to have upon the educational process are the provisions within the Act which require schools to make available to parents more detailed information about secondary schools and accord them strengthened rights over the choice of their child's school. The likely consequence of such measures is that some schools will develop a reputation as highly desirable. This effectively will act as a *self-fulfilling prophecy*, since more middle-class parents (whose children continue to produce better results in terms of measured academic outcomes) will opt for them. This is a good example of how the shape of educational provision can be significantly changed without any 'policy' in the formal, overt sense, being made or implemented. Similarly teachers, by their actions in the classroom and through their exercise of professional judgements, routinely make and implement social policy in and through education.

The complexities of the relationships of power and control between different parties to educational policy-making and implementation were well illustrated by the dispute at the William Tyndale junior school in London in 1975. Accounts of these events have been given by two journalists, by the teachers who were at the centre of the dispute, and in the Auld report, the official ILEA enquiry into the case. Briefly, the dispute was about the way the school was organised and the 'informal' style of education being offered. Complaints from parents and from some members of staff occasioned several governors to become involved, then subsequently officials and elected members of the LEA. The episode was well publicised in the media, which linked it with the themes of the Black Papers. Finally, after a formal enquiry set up by the LEA, four of the teachers, including the head, were dismissed.

There are many fascinating aspects to this case but, from the point of view of issues of power and control within the educational system, perhaps the most interesting is that the whole affair was protracted and confused. Teachers, parents, governors and inspectors all held differing views about what constitutes satisfactory education and who should ultimately decide what goes on in the classroom. The complexities of the division of powers and responsibilities within the English system assume – and to some extent require – that there is broad consensus between parties for most of the time. Where the different parties do *not* agree (as in the Tyndale case) there is certainly no easy mechanism for resolving the issue and the disruptive consequence can be fairly spectacular. Ultimate power of course is held by those bodies (usually either the LEA or the Secretary of State) who have the legal powers to dismiss teachers, modify the character of schools, and so on. The most important lesson to be learned from the Tyndale case . . . is that one can never assume that policy in education is unproblematically 'made' and then straightforwardly 'happens' at grassroots level. The many steps between, say, the passing of a piece of legislation in Parliament and what actually happens in the local primary school on a Monday morning, leaves ample room for 'policy' to be interpreted, adapted, fought over and sometimes effectively ignored. Social policy in education (as in other fields of welfare) is very much a contested arena.

J. Finch, *Education as Social Policy*, 1984, pp. 57–9.

Questions
1. *What do you understand by 'self-fulfilling prophecy' (para. 2)? Explain the way in which Janet Finch uses this term.*
2. *Do you agree with Finch's view that consensus is assumed between the groups involved in the English school system? Give reasons for your answer.*
3. *Examine the relationship between power and control in any recent educational event concerning policy-making (e.g. local events might include plans for school reorganisation, national events might include negotiations between the DES and the teachers' unions).*

COMPREHENSIVE SCHOOLS AND EDUCATIONAL INEQUALITY

As we have seen in previous chapters, educational inequality is one of the central issues with which sociologists have been concerned. Caroline Benn highlights some of the problems involved in achieving equality of educational opportunity and promoting equality in comprehensive schools. She criticises the examination system which is to be reformed in the late 1980s.

Reading 2

The case history of comprehensive reorganization reads like a fever chart: plans in, plans cancelled; reorganization begun, selection craftily reintroduced; refusal to budge, followed by a rush to catch up. Despite the failure at the top to guide and decide, and the lack of definition in every area of comprehensive practice, political opponents of equality continued to harp on the imposition of uniformity. The truth was the reverse. Variety was so rampant that comprehensive practice could almost be defined as being whatever your own local comprehensive happened to be doing at any given time. All the more remarkable, therefore, that a commonality of practice developed spontaneously, when, from the first, comprehensives were left to decide how to combine the old 'grammar' and 'modern' sides into something new. A few schools retained the sides separately, but most started their own common course: the same curriculum for all their pupils up to thirteen-plus. Even so, many with a common course still streamed it at first, or introduced setting for some subjects, to prepare for GCE selection after thirteen-plus.

By the mid-1970s, however, the majority of comprehensives had many mixed-ability classes, which only increased pressure for access to GCE courses in the higher forms. GCE was still seen as the 'quality' course which counted; and the majority were still excluded – as they had been from the grammar schools after 1944. They took the newer CSE examination or nothing at all. Even here there was no standard practice: some schools were sitting all pupils in one or other of the two examinations, while others had up to 50 per cent on 'non-exam' courses. For older pupils some comprehensive systems could offer only eight subjects at A-level, others up to twenty-eight. The fact that so many teachers were prepared to argue that CSE was a better sixteen-plus examination for most subjects for most pupils (and that A-level was narrow, cluttered and overdue for reform) made GCE selection inside comprehensives even harder to justify.

Thus within schools the retention of the grammar examination system of GCE became as big an obstacle to equality of educational opportunity as was the retention of grammar selection between schools. Support for an end to both types of selection and for a truly common assessment system at sixteen-plus and a new system at eighteen-plus, met head-on Conservative opposition and a Labour Government's irresolution in the face of continuing political difficulties in executing the reform. Thus the new comprehensives – with less than their fair share of GCE pupils – were given the impossible task of 'proving' themselves the GCE 'equal' of the grammar and private schools, while these privileged schools were still permitted to recruit only GCE pupils. Moreover, comprehensives had to 'prove' this in an atmosphere of high controversy and considerable prejudice, for, not unnaturally, the media were quick from the first to capitalize on the deeper political argument, and to side, on the whole, with privilege.

> C. Benn, 'Elites versus equals: the political background to the comprehensive reform', in D. Rubinstein (ed), *Education and Equality*, 1979, pp. 199–201.

Questions
1. *Examine the arguments for and against comprehensive education.*
2. *Why do you think Caroline Benn sees the GCE examination as an obstacle to equality of educational opportunity?*
3. *How far has equality of educational opportunity been achieved in your local education authority?*

POSITIVE DISCRIMINATION AND THE SCHOOL CURRICULUM

In recent years a range of policies have been introduced in order to prevent social and educational disadvantage. Many policies attempt to overcome the barriers to high attainment by the disadvantaged. Among the areas considered for possible action is the school curriculum. Mortimore and Blackstone evaluate a range of curriculum developments.

Reading 3

There seems little doubt that many of the curriculum developments considered to be of potential benefit for disadvantaged pupils have resulted in '*two nations*' within one school. But the problem of how to interest and motivate some groups of pupils taxes many teachers and is not solved by offering the traditional academic curriculum to all. It is argued by Smith (1979) that the basis of the present curriculum in the majority of secondary schools is historical rather than rational and that decisions affecting ways in which knowledge is classified into discrete subjects or in which certain knowledge is considered 'acceptable' are quite arbitrary. Smith supports Bernstein's (1971) contention that only rarely is the 'ultimate mystery of the subject' attained. This means that many are doomed to frustration, disappointment or to divisive dual curricula which contribute to the alienation of many, in particular the less able pupils. Smith also accepts Bruner's claim that most things can be taught to most pupils in a 'philosophically and conceptually coherent manner' and he argues that unless schools offer a broad common experience 'equality of opportunity is a meaningless phrase'. The *aims* of education should be the same for all pupils even if the *content* could not be the same for varied groups of pupils for 'unless we accept the fact that all children are entitled to the same broad types of experience and unless we try to develop in them all the same broad types of understanding, we are perpetuating a recipe for individual dissatisfaction and social unrest' (Smith).

Shipman's view, and that expressed in the HMI Primary Survey is that there is a lack of sequence and continuity at all stages of learning (between subjects, between one school and the next and between schooling and education outside school). Further, Shipman argues, there is resistance to organising for continuity, exemplified in the reactions of some nursery teachers in the EPA projects to the use of the Peabody Language Development Kit. Citing from Tizard that there was no evidence of the long-term impact of pre-schooling, Shipman suggests that this is not surprising since there was no 'apparent commitment to using nursery schooling for systematically building a base for later attainment' (Shipman, 1980).

The initial success of some of the structured learning programmes such as the Follow Through Planned Variations Programme suggests the value of structure and organisation in both intervention programmes and mainstream schooling rather than the inefficient 'ad hoc' approaches described by Hilsum and Cane (1971) and Taylor (1973).

A systematic approach to education is crucial for disadvantaged pupils who may find it harder to cope with 'discovery methods' that depend on the child 'being able to find the necessary human and material resources . . . middle-class parents support child-centred schooling because they teach the basic skills at home' (Shipman). This is a view supported by Bernstein in his discussion of the 'invisible pedagogy' in infant schools, by Tizard in her plea for the development of a nursery curriculum, and by Sharp and Green in their study of an East End primary school.

To conclude, complex educational problems, many of which have their roots in social and economic problems, are unlikely to be solved by single solutions in the form of one-off small investment programmes. Sustained reinforcement is necessary. Specially designed programmes may be able to attain specific objectives but no programme is likely to have a deep and lasting impact if it is not a planned part of the mainstream of education.

J. Mortimore and T. Blackstone, *Disadvantage and Education*, 1982, pp. 137–8.

Questions

1. *Do curriculum developments for the disadvantaged result in 'two nations' (para. 1) within a school? Give reasons for your answer.*
2. *Assess the view that a systematic approach to education is required for disadvantaged pupils.*
3. *Do programmes for the disadvantaged need to be part of mainstream education? Give reasons for your answer.*

A POLICY RESPONSE TO BLACK PUPILS

Much research on policy-making has focused on relationships between central authority, local authority and schools. In this reading, Barry Troyna highlights central–local relations in an analysis of policy issues on black pupils. He not only examines decision-making processes but the ways in which they are justified.

Reading 4

The educational response to black pupils in British schools has not been orchestrated by centrally prescribed policies, but has originated largely from the initiatives taken by LEAs and individual schools. One of the principal ways in which the DES has justified its decision not to prepare a uniform policy on this issue has been to stress its own lack of authority in a decentralised education system. It has argued that the formulation of a 'coherent and practical policy' at central government level would encroach on the 'freedom' and 'autonomy' of LEAs and undermine the diffusion of responsibility for policy decisions enshrined in the 1944 Education Act. In 1974, for example, the following response to the Select Committee's recommendation for the setting up of a central fund to which LEAs could apply 'for resources to meet the special educational needs' of black pupils and their parents was published.

> The public provision of education is, for the most part, the responsibility of the local education authorities. It is financed like any other local authority service largely through the rates and Rate Support Grant. It is the job of the local authority to decide how best to use its resources of staff and money to meet the needs of its area. If specific grants for particular aspects of education in which the local authorities have previously enjoyed discretion were to be introduced,

the effect might be to reduce the scope of local responsibility (Home Office, 1974: 13–14).

Not only does this response highlight the ambivalence about central and local government relationships, it also suggests that the power to formulate educational policy rests ultimately with LEAs. This representation of DES authority is not however entirely accurate; local authorities are not 'free' or 'autonomous' and neither are their schools. Indeed, from 1960 onwards there have been moves to reassert some central influence over educational policy generally, and the curriculum in particular. The 1977 Green Paper clearly stipulated that whilst the responsibility for education is shared between the DES, LEAs and teachers, the distribution of power between them is neither static nor necessarily equable; it also indicated that a more positive approach from DES was to be characteristic of future policy:

> The Secretaries of State are responsible in law for the promotion of the education of the people of England and Wales. They need to know what is happening in the schools. *They must draw attention to national needs if they believe the education system is not adequately meeting them* (DES, 1977: 5, para. I.14, emphasis added).

Claims of institutional powerlessness therefore are largely untenable, and are certainly not sufficient to account for the reluctance of the DES to prescribe a 'coherent and practical policy' on the education of black pupils. Far more significant is its commitment to assimilation and a conception of the society as indivisible. Further, it insists that the cultural values and assumptions which underpin the society are non-negotiable. In refusing to formulate a policy based on the principle of multiculturalism, the DES acknowledges its reluctance, which is shared with central government, to concede any institutional or political power to the black communities. In the absence of negotiation and concession, and the continued pre-eminence of assimilation as a characteristic of DES and LEA approaches to this issue, multiculturalism in education remains a myth:

> Is (Britain) a society in which the best is taken from, say, West Indian, Asian and English culture to form a basis for a new culture? Is it a society in which the English culture must adapt itself to new and increasingly powerful voices of the

different cultures? Are immigrant cultural forces sufficiently powerful to encourage the indigenous population to change its cultural heritage? Will a 'ghetto' situation contain immigrant cultures and cause the indigenous population to ignore and disregard immigrants, causing a multiracial society to remain really a racial one? (Head teacher cited in Townsend and Brittan, 1973: 16–17).

B. Troyna, 'The ideological and policy response to black pupils in British schools' in A. Hartnett (ed), *The Social Sciences in Educational Studies*, 1982, pp. 137–9.

Questions
1. *What does the policy response to black pupils tell us about patterns of decision-making in the English educational system?*
2. *What is multiculturalism?*
3. *Is multiculturalism a myth in English education?*

EDUCATION AND THE ERADICATION OF SEXISM

In focusing on policy issues it is important to examine the social context in which they are located and the relationship between economic and political circumstances and social policy. Rosemary Deem examines these issues in the course of considering sexism in education.

Reading 5

One of the biggest threats to the reduction of sexism in education is that posed by fluctuations in the economy. Economic recessions, like the one experienced by Britain in the 1970s, can result in pressures for, and policies on, cuts in public expenditure. Since education in British society is a major area of expenditure, it is particularly vulnerable to public spending cuts. Although it may be argued that people's attitudes are of crucial importance to the existence or absence of sexism in schools, differentiation on grounds of sex is often based on unequal allocation and distribution of learning resources. Furthermore, sexism may be implicit in certain kinds of resources, such as reading materials or textbooks. If expenditure in schools is cut back, sexist reading schemes and other sexist literature may continue to be used, simply because non-sexist replacements are too expensive to purchase. Indeed, people may be discouraged from producing non-sexist literature because there is only a limited market for it. Children in primary schools may be forced to use play equipment which encourages sex-stereotyping because schools cannot afford to buy sufficient equipment for all children to choose which they use on the basis of interest. In secondary schools, shortages of money may mean that girls continue to be unable to make non-traditional choices of subject, such as sciences, technical subjects or mathematics, because not enough teachers or facilities are available for this to be possible. Similarly, boys may be prevented from taking arts subjects or domestic subjects.

In higher education the closure of colleges of education may well reduce the choice of courses available to women students with arts qualifications. Government initiatives on unemployment and training of school leavers for employment may also be affecting the post-school options available to girls. In further education the Manpower Services Commission (created in 1974 to provide public employment and training services), and one of the Commission's off-shoots, the Training Services Agency, which runs training schemes and courses, have both made considerable inroads into course and curriculum development and are becoming increasingly important in the financing of higher education. Since few of the people involved in the Commission or its agencies are women, and since most of the courses being provided under its auspices are technical, vocational and industrially-oriented ones which require scientific, technical or mathematical skills, girls are unlikely to benefit substantially from this involvement of the Commission in further education, and may well have their chances of taking courses suited to their interests and existing qualifications reduced. The Job Creation Scheme, which is a Government sponsored body helping to provide temporary work for the young unemployed, has also not favoured girl school leavers in its schemes, and about 76 per cent of the jobs in their programme up to 1977 were intended for boys. Girl school leavers then, are likely to find their chances of continuing their education or entering a worthwhile job hampered not only by their sex and school background in arts subjects, but also by the effects of the economic recession.

Can anything be done about all this? The existing legislation on women's rights and sex discrimination does not appear to have the breadth to cope with many of these problems, partly because the procedures for making complaints are based on individual cases, whereas the problems are often general ones. Furthermore, the Equal Opportunities Commission, the major official body concerned with implementing the British legislation on sex equality, has also suffered from the economic recession and the unwillingness of many to take the question of women's equality seriously in the face of what are seen as more pressing economic and political problems. But there is also the further difficulty that some problems of sexism in schools seem to lie beyond the scope of legislation. Whilst it would be possible to legally require schools to provide equal resources, equipment, and teachers for both sexes, our existing educational system would make the financing of these things difficult to arrange. Under the present system of block rate-support grant allocation to local authorities by central government, it is not possible to insist that money is spent on any particular item of expenditure.

R. Deem, *Women and Schooling*, 1978, pp. 128–9.

Questions
1. *Assess Rosemary Deem's view that 'one of the biggest threats to the reduction of sexism in education is that posed by fluctuations in the economy' (para. 1).*
2. *Examine current government policy in higher and further education. To what extent is Deem's analysis useful in your interpretation of the policy?*
3. *On the basis of sociological evidence outline a policy for eradicating sexism in education.*

SCHOOL LIFE AND WORK LIFE

Among the major educational events in the 1970s was the 'Great Debate' in education which was initiated by James Callaghan (the Prime Minister) in a speech given at Ruskin College, Oxford. A central concern was the relationship between school and industry and the content of the school curriculum which was discussed in many subsequent government documents.

Reading 6

In his Ruskin speech the Prime Minister gave special emphasis to the contribution that education has to make to the nation's industrial and commercial well-being. His concern about the relevance of present-day education to the needs of industry and commerce was reflected in many of the comments about this aspect of schools education at the regional conferences. It was said that the school system is geared to promote the importance of academic learning and careers with the result that pupils, especially the more able, are prejudiced against work in productive industry and trade; that teachers lack experience, knowledge and understanding of trade and industry; that curricula are not related to the realities of most pupils' work after leaving school; and that pupils leave school with little or no understanding of the workings, or importance, of the wealth-producing sector of our economy.

But there were many equally-strongly expressed criticisms directed at industry: for instance that employers often lay down unrealistic standards of attainment for school leavers well beyond what the job requires; that they have not made allowances for the fact that they are selecting from a group of school leavers which is more highly creamed by higher and further education than it would have been two decades ago. And overlying these specific comments was the frequently-expressed view that if certain occupations are perceived by young people as unattractive, it is unreasonable to expect teachers alone to remove the antipathy. If more able young people are to be persuaded to make their careers in industry and commerce the remedy lies with the companies and firms and only to a minor degree with the schools.

Manifestly there is a lack of understanding and communication. But the picture is not altogether gloomy; there was encouraging evidence at the regional conferences that some education authorities were already pioneering admirable schemes, including opportunities for visits between industry and schools and working parties to discuss common difficulties, for example in mathematics. And on a national scale there are some encouraging activities: the Schools Council Industry Project, and the Understanding British Industry project of the Confederation of British Industry (CBI). Some of the proposals put forward earlier in the sections on curriculum and teacher training will make a contribution here too.

But the key to better understanding lies above all with local initiative. There is no lack of possibilities. For example:

(i) People with experience in management and trades unions can be appointed as governors of schools.

(ii) Industry and commerce should be involved in the curriculum planning processes at national and local level, to ensure that their points of view are taken into account.

(iii) Employers and trades unions, through their first hand experience of industry and commerce, can make significant contributions to careers education and to improving understanding of productive industry by offering opportunities for work experience and work observation. Every effort should be made to make full use of such activities and relate them properly to school programmes.

(iv) Employers can offer serving and potential teachers opportunities to gain experience of working in industry. They can also foster direct contacts between their own staffs and teachers in local schools, and those in education should encourage employers to participate in this way.

(v) These contacts should be planned in particular to widen the career horizons of women. A much wider range and variety of job opportunities is now available to women.

(vi) For pupils continuing their education, liaison between schools and universities and polytechnics can help to develop subject interest and open possibilities for further study. This is especially relevant to engineering which, while it is not generally taught in schools, is of obvious industrial and national importance. Manufacturing industry recruits some 80% of its graduates from amongst engineering, science and technology graduates, and there has been a shortage of the most able school-leavers applying to take such courses, particularly engineering.

(vii) Close liaison between schools and colleges of further education is valuable, especially for pupils in their final statutory year in school. Before leaving school every young man and woman should have the opportunity to visit the local further education college to see the range of opportunities it offers and, wherever possible, should receive information about courses available.

(viii) Pupils should have the opportunity, where appropriate, of taking part in linked courses. The Government are encouraged by the development of co-operative efforts of this kind by national and regional bodies.

Young people need to reach maturity with a basic understanding of the economy and the activities, especially manufacturing industry, which are necessary for the creation of Britain's national wealth. It is an important task of secondary schools to develop this understanding, and opportunities for its development should be offered to pupils of all abilities. These opportunities are needed not only by young people who may have careers in industry later but perhaps even more by those who may work elsewhere, so that the role of industry becomes soundly appreciated by society in general.

It is for local education authorities, schools and industry to get together and decide which proposals best suit them: this is an area where no amount of central direction can take the place of local initiatives.

HMSO, *Education in Schools: A Consultative Document*, 1977, pp. 34–5.

Questions
1. *Critically evaluate the assumptions made about school life and work life in this extract.*
2. *What does this document tell you about educational decision-making in the English school system?*
3. *Write a commentary on this document from (i) a functionalist and (ii) a Marxist perspective.*

INDUSTRY AND EDUCATION: A CONTINUING DEBATE

Sociologists have taken much interest in the 'Great Debate' and have been active in analysing the events surrounding it and the responses that have been made. John Beck draws together some of the material that is available to make a preliminary assessment of education in the early 1980s.

Reading 7

The 1977 Green Paper had to be repeatedly re-drafted to satisfy the conflicting demands of those like the Prime Minister who 'took an active part in getting the Green Paper shortened and toughened up' (TES, 8th July, 1977, p. 1) as against those like Mr Hattersley and Mrs Williams herself, who apparently feared that the government would be presenting educational reactionaries 'with a whole new arsenal of anti-comprehensive weapons' (TES, 24th June, 1977, p. 80). In its final form, of course, the Green Paper had implications which went far wider than the debate about comprehensive schools. It systematically endorsed a clearly instrumental view of education as a means of engendering the transformation of attitudes which employers had been demanding, and it called for appropriate changes both in the school curriculum and in the training of teachers.

It was followed up by a series of policy initiatives (in which the DES and HMI played a much more prominent role than hitherto), for example, the Curriculum Review initiated by circular 14/77; the expansion of the role of the Assessment of Performance Unit; the restructuring of the Schools' Council in such a way as to reduce the influence of teachers' representatives; the establishment of the Department of Industry's Industry/ Education Unit in 1978 and of the associated Industry/Education Advisory Committee in 1979.

It is still too soon to attempt any overall assessment of the effects of these developments; as Esland and Cathcart have noted, 'there are few studies of the actual influence of industry within educational policy making' (Esland and Cathcart, 1981, p. 93). Preliminary indications, however, suggest that the impact of these attempts to change the content of education in schools and in teacher training institutions has been uneven. Whitty's research on school examinations indicates that as far as the curriculum of those pupils who take *GCE* examinations is concerned, the university-dominated GCE examination boards have successfully resisted the industrial lobby and have 'ensured the maintenance of a more significant place for old humanist conceptions of a liberal secondary education than might have been predicted from the sort of attacks on the traditional school curriculum that emanated from the representatives of government and industry in the opening stages of the Great Debate' (Whitty, 1983, p. 181). For the non-elite, the situation appears to be rather different. Here, concern about chronic and large-scale youth unemployment has helped to produce a situation in which a substantial number of teachers appear to have been persuaded, at least to some extent, that the kinds of curriculum change called for in the Green Paper and subsequent documents are necessary and should be introduced. Such sentiments have been reinforced by the fact that school examination certificates, particularly CSEs, now have little currency on the labour market and are therefore less effective as a source of extrinsic motivation. For these reasons, it has been claimed that the traditional curriculum has failed the 'average 16 year old' largely because it is too academic and irrelevant to the real world which such pupils will now have to face when they leave school.

> J. Beck, 'Accountability, industry and education: reflections on
> some aspects of the educational and industrial practices of the
> Labour administration of 1974–9' in J. Ahier and M. Flude (eds),
> *Contemporary Education Policy*, 1983, pp. 226–7.

Questions

1. *Do you agree with John Beck's view that the Green Paper provides an instrumental view of education? Give reasons for your answer.*
2. *How would you account for the fact that the GCE examinations have resisted the industrial lobby?*
3. *Has the traditional curriculum failed 'the average 16 year old'? Give reasons for your answer.*

RESOURCING EDUCATION: THE EFFECT OF PUBLIC EXPENDITURE CUTS

All educational decisions and educational policy-making occurs in a political context. In recent years decisions about educational spending have had a direct impact upon schools and the educational services that can be provided. In this reading, HMI provide an assessment of the effect of public expenditure cuts.

Reading 8

To put it in a nutshell, many LEAs and schools are surviving financially by doing less; but they are often obliged to take the less in the form that comes easily to hand rather than shaping it to match educational priorities. This means, in some cases, a general retrenchment in which most services, schools and pupils are affected to some degree. But it is clear that some things are more vulnerable than others. Subjects that require expensive specialist books or materials and equipment for practical work, and which are taken by relatively few pupils, are particularly at risk. Remedial teaching, courses for academically less able pupils and additional work with the very able, are less easy to justify and provide when provision for the majority is under pressure. Except in those LEAs with well organised policies of positive discrimination, schools and pupils in deprived and disadvantaged areas are adversely affected by a combination of factors including old and deteriorating buildings, sharp falls in pupil numbers, reductions in specialist help for pupils with learning difficulties, cuts in ancillary staff, such as nursery assistants and classroom helpers, and the absence of alternative sources of funding from, and support within, the community.

Schools are turning increasingly to parents and the local community for financial and other help. Some schools have a long tradition of raising funds to pay for educational visits and desirable but expensive items of equipment. Funds are now frequently used to provide basic materials and equipment. This trend is leading to marked disparities of provision between schools serving affluent and poor areas.

> HMI, *The Effects of Local Authority Expenditure Policies on the Education Service in England, 1981*, 1982, paragraphs 72–3.

Questions
1. *Using the evidence in this reading, identify the main trends in public expenditure cuts and comment upon their sociological significance.*
2. *What conclusions can be drawn from the findings of this report? What are their social implications?*
3. *Discuss the way in which you would conduct sociological research on the effects of public expenditure cuts in your school or college.*

ESSAY QUESTIONS
1. Have post-war changes in educational policy and provision brought Britain closer to realising the 'vision' of a meritocratic society? (AEB, 1983)
2. Critically evaluate educational policy on *either* the relationship between school and work *or* the school curriculum in England in the last ten years.
3. 'Educational policy in the United Kingdom has not resulted in equality of educational opportunity.' Discuss.
4. Outline and discuss the relationship between educational politics and educational policy in post-war Britain.

FURTHER READING
Many contemporary educational events concerning politics and policy are reviewed and discussed in *The Times Educational Supplement* and *New Society*, which have source materials that can be evaluated from a sociological perspective.

1. J. Ahier and M. Flude (eds), *Contemporary Education Policy*, Croom Helm, 1983.

   A useful collection of papers that survey current policies from a sociological perspective. The volume begins with a useful review of the history and sociology of educational policy.

2. T. Bush and M. Kogan, *Directors of Education*, Allen and Unwin, 1982.

   Contains interviews with directors of education. It is very readable.

3. B. Cosin and M. Hales (eds), *Educational Policy and Society: Theoretical Perspectives*, Routledge and Kegan Paul, 1983.

   Part four on policy and ideology is especially useful, containing papers on middle schools, the education of women and the Manpower Services Commission.

4. J. Finch, *Education as Social Policy*, Longman, 1984.

   A short readable guide to this field of study. Part one is especially useful on a social policy outline of English education since 1944.

5. M. Kogan, *Educational Policy Making*, Allen and Unwin, 1975.

   A useful discussion of policy-making in English education.

6. M. Kogan, *The Politics of Educational Change*, Fontana, 1978.

   The second section is particularly useful on the curriculum.

7. D. Lawton, *The Politics of the School Curriculum*, Routledge and Kegan Paul, 1980.

   Contains a useful review of the major curriculum issues in the 1970s and addresses the question of who controls the school curriculum.

8. P. Lodge and T. Blackstone, *Educational Policy and Educational Inequality*, Martin Robertson, 1982.

   Contains a good analysis of policy-makers, especially in relation to nursery education, positive discrimination, selection at eleven, raising the school-leaving age and higher education.

9. J. Mortimore and T. Blackstone, *Disadvantage and Education*, Heinemann, 1982.

   The discussion of positive discrimination and policies to alleviate educational disadvantage (chs 4 and 5) are particularly good.

10. B. Salter and T. Tapper, *Education, Politics and the State: The Theory and Practice of Educational Change*, Grant McIntyre, 1981.

    The case studies in the second part of the book, dealing with educational power and issues concerning education and industry, intelligence testing and the public schools, are useful.

List of readings

CHAPTER 1

E. Durkheim, *Education and Sociology* (New York: Free Press, 1956) pp. 67–9.

K. Harris, *Teachers and Classes: A Marxist Analysis* (London: Routledge and Kegan Paul, 1982) pp. 7–8.

J. Evetts, *The Sociology of Educational Ideas* (London: Routledge and Kegan Paul, 1973), p. 123.

P. Gordon and D. Lawton, *Curriculum Change in the Nineteenth and Twentieth Centuries* (London: Hodder and Stoughton, 1978) p. 129.

B. Williamson, *Education, Social Structure and Development* (London: Macmillan, 1979), pp. 161–3.

B. Jackson, 'A question of equality' in J. E. C. MacBeath (ed), *A Question of Schooling* (London: Hodder and Stoughton, 1976) pp. 21–2.

School of Barbiana, *Letter to a Teacher* (Harmondsworth: Penguin, 1970) pp. 18–20.

I. Lister, 'The concept of deschooling and the future of secondary education' in I. Lister (ed), *Deschooling: A Reader* (Cambridge University Press, 1974) pp. 89–90.

CHAPTER 2

R. Dore, *The Diploma Disease: Education, Qualification and Development* (London: Allen and Unwin, 1976) pp. 14–15.

J. Karabel and A. H. Halsey (eds), *Power and Ideology in Education* (Oxford University Press, 1977) pp. 8–9.

M. Sanderson, *The Universities and British Industry* (London: Routledge and Kegan Paul, 1972) pp. 362–3.

S. Bowles and H. Gintis, *Schooling in Capitalist America* (London: Routledge and Kegan Paul, 1976) pp. 131–2.

D. Finn and S. Frith, 'Education and the labour market' in Open University, *The State and the Politics of Education*, Block 1, Part 2, Unit 4, (Milton Keynes: Open University Press, 1981) pp. 48–9.

P. Willis, *Learning to Labour* (Farnborough: Saxon House, 1977) pp. 91–2.

H. Roberts, 'After sixteen: what choice?' in R. G. Burgess (ed), *Exploring Society* (London: British Sociological Association, 1982) pp. 108–9. The data originally appeared in H. Roberts and M. Sharp, *After Sixteen: What Happens to the Girls?* (Bradford Metropolitan District, 1982).

B. Main and D. Raffe, 'The "transition from school to work" in 1980/81:

180

a dynamic account', in *British Educational Research Journal*, vol. 9, no. 1 (1983) 61, Table 1 (adapted).

CHAPTER 3

R. H. Tawney, *Equality*, 5th edn (London: Allen and Unwin, 1964; originally published 1931) pp. 142–4.

A. H. Halsey, A. F. Heath and J. M. Ridge, *Origins and Destinations: Family, Class and Education in Modern Britain* (Oxford University Press, 1980) pp. 201–3.

T. Blackstone, 'Falling short of meritocracy', *The Times Higher Education Supplement*, 18 January 1980, p. 14.

J. H. Ballantine, *The Sociology of Education: A Systematic Analysis* (Englewood Cliffs, New Jersey: Prentice-Hall, 1983) pp. 86–8.

R. H. Turner, 'Sponsored and contest mobility and the school system' in A. H. Halsey, J. Floud and C. A. Anderson (eds), *Education, Economy and Society* (New York: Free Press, 1961) pp. 135–7.

A. H. Halsey, 'Social mobility and education' in D. Rubinstein (ed), *Education and Equality* (Harmondsworth: Penguin, 1979) pp. 61–2.

I. Payne, 'A working class girl in a grammar school' in D. Spender and E. Sarah (eds), *Learning to Lose: Sexism and Education* (London: The Women's Press, 1980) pp. 16–18.

J. Westergaard and H. Resler, *Class in a Capitalist Society* (Harmondsworth: Penguin, 1976) pp. 340–2.

CHAPTER 4

A. H. Halsey, A. F. Heath and J. M. Ridge, *Origins and Destinations* (Oxford University Press, 1980) based on Table 8.12, p. 142.

Social Trends 1984 (London: HMSO, 1983) chart 3.7, p. 47.

Rampton Committee, *West Indian Children in Our Schools* (London: HMSO, 1981) Tables C and D, p. 8.

J. W. B. Douglas, J. M. Ross and H. R. Simpson, *All Our Future* (London: Panther, 1971) pp. 196–200.

R. K. Brown, 'Introduction', in R. K. Brown (ed), *Knowledge, Education and Cultural Change* (London: Tavistock, 1973) p. 5.

M. Stubbs, *Language, Schools and Classrooms*, 2nd edn (London: Methuen, 1983) pp. 59–61.

R. Walden and V. Walkerdine, *Girls and Mathematics: the Early Years, Bedford Way Papers No. 8* (London: University of London, Institute of Education, 1982) pp. 61–3.

D. Byrne, B. Williamson and B. Fletcher, *The Poverty of Education: A Study in the Politics of Opportunity* (Oxford: Martin Robertson, 1975) pp. 165–6.

CHAPTER 5

R. G. Burgess, *Experiencing Comprehensive Education: A Study of Bishop McGregor School* (London: Methuen, 1983) pp. 43–5.

R. King, *The Sociology of School Organization* (London: Methuen, 1983) pp. 40–2.

D. H. Hargreaves, *Social Relations in a Secondary School* (London: Routledge and Kegan Paul, 1967) pp. 172–3.

C. Lacey, *Hightown Grammar: The School as a Social System* (Manchester University Press, 1970) pp. 57–8.

D. Newbold, *Ability Grouping – the Banbury Enquiry* (Slough: National Foundation for Educational Research, 1977) pp. 110–11.

S. J. Ball, *Beachside Comprehensive: A Case Study of Secondary Schooling* (Cambridge University Press, 1981) pp. 288–90.

M. Rutter, B. Maughan, P. Mortimore and J. Ouston, *Fifteen Thousand Hours; Secondary Schools and Their Effects on Children* (London: Open Books, 1979) pp. 180–2.

D. Reynolds, 'Review symposium: *Fifteen Thousand Hours*', *British Journal of Sociology of Education*, vol. 1, no. 2 (1980) 209–10.

CHAPTER 6

S. J. Ball, 'Initial encounters in the classroom and the process of establishment', in P. Woods (ed), *Pupil Strategies: Explorations in the Sociology of the School* (London: Croom Helm, 1980) pp. 146–8.

A. D. Edwards and V. J. Furlong, *The Language of Teaching* (London: Heinemann, 1978) pp. 83–5.

D. H. Hargreaves, S. K. Hester and F. J. Mellor, *Deviance in Classrooms* (London: Routledge and Kegan Paul, 1975) pp. 146–7.

P. Woods, *The Divided School* (London: Routledge and Kegan Paul, 1979) pp. 155–7.

S. Delamont, *Interaction in the Classroom*, 2nd edn (London: Methuen, 1983) pp. 105–7.

R. G. Burgess, *Experiencing Comprehensive Education: A Study of Bishop McGregor School* (London: Methuen, 1983) pp. 217–20.

M. Stanworth, *Gender and Schooling: A Study of Sexual Divisions in the Classroom* (London: Women's Research and Resources Centre, 1981) pp. 36–7.

M. Fuller, 'Black girls in a London comprehensive school', in R. Deem (ed), *Schooling for Women's Work* (London: Routledge and Kegan Paul, 1980) pp. 59–61.

CHAPTER 7

M. F. D. Young, 'An approach to the study of curricula as socially organised knowledge', in M. F. D. Young (ed), *Knowledge and Control: New Directions for the Sociology of Education* (London: Collier-Macmillan, 1971) pp. 31–2.

C. Norwood, *Curriculum and Examinations in Secondary Schools* (London: HMSO, 1943) p. 4.

N. Keddie, 'Classroom knowledge', in M. F. D. Young (ed), *Knowledge and Control: New Directions for the Sociology of Education* (London: Collier-Macmillan, 1971) pp. 147–8.

I. F. Goodson, *School Subjects and Curriculum Change* (London: Croom Helm, 1982) pp. 82–3.

R. G. Burgess, 'It's not a proper subject: it's just Newsom', in I. F. Goodson and S. J. Ball (eds), *Defining the Curriculum* (Lewes: Falmer Press, 1984) pp. 190–2.

D. H. Hargreaves, *The Challenge for the Comprehensive School: Culture, Curriculum and Community* (London: Routledge and Kegan Paul, 1982) pp. 63–4.

J. Samuel, 'Feminism and science teaching: some classroom observations', in A. Kelly (ed), *The Missing Half: Girls and Science Education* (Manchester University Press, 1981) pp. 252–3.

Department of Education and Science, *Curricular Differences for Boys and Girls* (London: HMSO, 1975) Table 7, p. 13.

CHAPTER 8

J. Finch, *Education as Social Policy* (London: Longman, 1984) pp. 57–9.

C. Benn, 'Elites versus equals: the political background to the comprehensive reform', in D. Rubinstein (ed), *Education and Equality*, (Harmondsworth: Penguin, 1979) pp. 199–201.

J. Mortimore and T. Blackstone, *Disadvantage and Education* (London: Heinemann, 1982) pp. 137–8.

B. Troyna, 'The ideological and policy response to black pupils in British schools' in A. Hartnett (ed), *The Social Sciences in Educational Studies* (London: Heinemann, 1982) pp. 137–9.

R. Deem, *Women and Schooling* (London: Routledge and Kegan Paul, 1978) pp. 128–9.

HMSO, *Education in Schools: A Consultative Document*, Cmnd 6869 (London: HMSO, 1977) pp. 34–5.

J. Beck, 'Accountability, industry and education: reflections on some aspects of the educational and industrial practices of the Labour administration of 1974–79' in J. Ahier and M. Flude (eds), *Contemporary Education Policy* (London: Croom Helm, 1983) pp. 226–7.

HMI, *The Effects of Local Authority Expenditure Policies on the Education Service in England, 1981* (London: HMSO, 1982) paragraphs 72–3.

Bibliography

Note: The following list includes all material that is referred to in the text but does not repeat items that are only listed in the suggestions for further reading at the end of each chapter.

R. Aronson, 'Is busing the real issue?', *Dissent*, vol. 25 (1978).

E. Ashby, 'On universities and the scientific revolution', in A. H. Halsey, J. Floud and C. A. Anderson (eds), *Education, Economy and Society* (New York: Free Press, 1961) pp. 466–76.

D. N. Ashton and M. J. Maguire, 'The function of academic and non-academic criteria in employers' selection strategies', *British Journal of Guidance and Counselling*, vol. 8, no. 2 (1980) 146–57.

S. J. Ball, *Beachside Comprehensive: A Case Study of Secondary Schooling* (Cambridge University Press, 1981).

J. Beck *et al.*, *Worlds Apart: Readings for a Sociology of Education* (London: Collier-Macmillan, 1976).

B. Bernstein, 'On the classification and framing of educational knowledge' in M. F. D. Young (ed), *Knowledge and Control: New Directions for the Sociology of Education* (London: Collier-Macmillan, 1971) pp. 47–69.

B. Bernstein, *Class, Codes and Control*, vol. 3 (London: Routledge and Kegan Paul, 1975).

S. Bowles and H. Gintis, *Schooling in Capitalist America* (London: Routledge and Kegan Paul, 1976).

R. G. Burgess (ed), *The Research Process in Educational Settings: Ten Case Studies* (Lewes: Falmer Press, 1984).

E. M. Byrne, 'Inequality in education – discriminal resouce-allocation in schools', *Educational Review*, vol. 27, no. 3 (1975) 179–91.

B. R. Clark, *Educating the Expert Society* (San Francisco: Chandler, 1962).

M. Cole, 'Contradictions in the educational theory of Gintis and Bowles', *Sociological Review*, vol. 31, no. 3 (1983) 471–88.

J. S. Coleman *et al.*, *Report on Equality of Educational Opportunity* (Washington: US Government Printing Office, 1966).

B. Davies, *Social Control and Education* (London: Methuen, 1976).

S. Delamont, *Interaction in the Classroom* (London: Methuen, 1976; 2nd edn 1983).

S. Delamont, 'All too familiar? A decade of classroom research', *Educational Analysis*, vol. 3, no. 1 (1981) 69–83.

Department of Education and Science, *Eduation in Schools: A Consultative Document*, Green Paper, Cmnd 6869 (London: HMSO, 1977).

G. M. Esland and H. Cathcart, *Education and the Corporate Economy*, Open University Course E353 Society, Education and the State, Block 1, Unit 2 (Milton Keynes: Open University Press, 1981).

K. Fogelman (ed), *Growing Up in Great Britain* (London: Macmillan, 1983).

D. Glass (ed), *Social Mobility* (London: Routledge and Kegan Paul, 1954).

J. Goldthorpe, *Social Mobility and Class Structure in Modern Britain* (Oxford: Clarendon Press, 1980).

I. F. Goodson and S. J. Ball (eds), *Defining the Curriculum* (Lewes: Falmer Press, 1984).

J. C. B. Gordon, *Verbal Deficit: A Critique* (London: Croom Helm, 1981).

A. H. Halsey, J. Floud and C. A. Anderson (eds), *Education, Economy and Society* (New York: Free Press, 1961).

A. H. Halsey, A. F. Heath and J. M. Ridge, *Origins and Destinations: Family, Class and Education in Modern Britain* (Oxford: Clarendon Press, 1980).

S. Hilsum and B. S. Cane, *The Teacher's Day* (Slough: NFER, 1971).

G. Hodgson, 'Inequality: do schools make a difference?' in H. Silver (ed), *Equal Opportunity in Education* (London: Methuen, 1973) pp. 352–67.

Home Office, *Educational Disadvantage and the Educational Needs of Immigrants: Observations on the Report on Education of the Select Committee on Race Relations and Immigration*, Cmnd 5720 (London: HMSO, 1974).

E. Hopper (ed), *Readings in the Theory of Educational Systems* (London: Hutchinson, 1971).

C. Jencks *et al.*, *Inequality: A Reassessment of the Effect of Family and Schooling in America* (London: Basic Books, 1972).

Joint Board of Pre-Vocational Education, *The Certificate of Pre-Vocational Education: Consultative Document* (London: Joint Board of Pre-Vocational Education, 1984).

J. Karabel and A. H. Halsey (eds), *Power and Ideology in Education* (Oxford University Press, 1977).

A. Kelly (ed), *The Missing Half: Girls and Science Education* (Manchester University Press, 1981).

R. A. King, *School Organisation and Pupil Involvement* (London: Routledge and Kegan Paul, 1973).

D. Lee and H. Newby, *The Problem of Sociology* (London: Hutchinson, 1983).

F. Musgrove, *School and the Social Order* (Chichester: Wiley, 1979).

J. Newsom, *Half Our Future* (Newsom Report), (London: HMSO, 1963).

I. Payne, 'A working class girl in a grammar school', in D. Spender and E. Sarah (eds), *Learning to Lose: Sexism and Education* (London: The Women's Press, 1980) pp. 12–19.

J. Purvis, 'The double burden of class and gender in the schooling of working class girls in nineteenth century England, 1800–1870', in L. Barton and S. Walker (eds), *Schools, Teachers and Teaching*

(Lewes: Falmer Press, 1981) pp. 97–116.

W. Quine, 'Polarized cultures in comprehensive schools', *Research in Education*, no. 12 (1974) 9–15.

A. Rampton, *West Indian Children in Our Schools* (London: HMSO, 1981).

D. Reader, 'A recurring debate: education and industry', in G. Bernbaum (ed), *Schooling in Decline* (London: Macmillan, 1979) pp. 115–48.

B. Salter and T. Tapper, *Education, Politics and the State: The Theory and Practice of Educational Change* (London: Grant McIntyre, 1981).

M. Shipman, 'The limits of positive discrimination', in M. Marland (ed), *Education for the Inner City* (London: Heinemann, 1980) pp. 69–92.

S. Smith, 'Slow learners and the secondary school curriculum', in D. Rubinstein (ed), *Education and Equality* (Harmondsworth: Penguin, 1979) pp. 176–90.

P. Stanworth, 'Elites and privilege' in P. Abrams and R. K. Brown (eds), *U. K. Society To-day: Work, Urbanism and Inequality*, 2nd edn (London: Weidenfeld and Nicholson, 1984).

B. Sugarman, 'Involvement in youth culture, academic achievement and conformity in school', *British Journal of Sociology*, vol. 18, no. 2 (1967) 151–64.

W. Taylor, *Heading for Change: Management of Innovation in the Large Secondary School* (London: Routledge and Kegan Paul, 1973).

R. H. Tawney, *Equality*, 5th edn (London: Allen and Unwin, 1964; originally published 1931).

S. Tomlinson, *Ethnic Minorities in British Schools: A Review of the Literature, 1960–82* (London: Heinemann, 1983).

H. E. R. Townsend and E. Brittan, *Multicultural Education: Need and Innovation*, Schools Council Working Paper 50 (London: Evans/Methuen, 1973).

W. Waller, *The Sociology of Teaching* (New York: Wiley, 1932).

A. G. Watts, *Education, Unemployment and the Future of Work* (Milton Keynes: Open University Press, 1983).

J. Webb, 'The sociology of a school', *British Journal of Sociology*, vol. 13, no. 3 (1962) 264–72.

H. Weinreich-Haste, 'What sex is science?' in O. Hartnett, G. Boden and M. Fuller (eds), *Sex-Role Stereotyping* (London: Tavistock, 1979) pp. 168–81.

C. Werthman, 'Delinquents in schools', *Berkeley Journal of Sociology*, vol. 8 (1963) 39–60; reprinted in B. Cosin *et al.*, *School and Society*, 2nd edn (London: Routledge and Kegan Paul, 1977).

G. Whitty, 'State policy and school examinations 1976–82: an exploration of some implications of the sixteen plus controversy', in J. Ahier and M. Flude (eds), *Contemporary Education Policy* (London: Croom Helm, 1983) pp. 165–90.

B. Williamson, 'Contradictions of control: elementary education in a mining district 1870–1977', in L. Barton and S. Walker (eds), *Schools, Teachers and Teaching* (Lewes: Falmer Press, 1981) pp. 77–95.

P. Woods, 'The myth of subject choice', *British Journal of Sociology*, vol. 27, no. 2 (1976) pp. 130–49.

P. Woods, *The Divided School* (London: Routledge and Kegan Paul, 1979).

A. Yates and D. Pidgeon, *Admission to Grammar Schools* (London: Newnes, 1957).

M. F. D. Young (ed), *Knowledge and Control: New Directions for the Sociology of Education* (London: Collier-Macmillan, 1971).

Index